Peter W. Rodgers

NATION, REGION AND HISTORY
IN POST-COMMUNIST TRANSITIONS

Identity Politics in Ukraine, 1991-2006

With a foreword by Vera Tolz

ibidem-Verlag
Stuttgart

Bibliografische Information der Deutschen Nationalbibliothek
Die Deutsche Nationalbibliothek verzeichnet diese Publikation in der
Deutschen Nationalbibliografie; detaillierte bibliografische Daten sind im
Internet über http://dnb.d-nb.de abrufbar.

Bibliographic information published by the Deutsche Nationalbibliothek
Die Deutsche Nationalbibliothek lists this publication in the Deutsche Nationalbibliografie;
detailed bibliographic data are available in the Internet at http://dnb.d-nb.de.

Frontcover picture: 'The monument to Lenin' situated on Theatre Square in the centre of
Luhans'k. Photographed by Peter W. Rodgers, April 2007.

∞

Gedruckt auf alterungsbeständigem, säurefreien Papier
Printed on acid-free paper

ISSN: 1614-3515

ISBN-10: 3-89821-903-8
ISBN-13: 978-3-89821-903-7

© *ibidem*-Verlag
Stuttgart 2008

Printed in Germany

Soviet and Post-Soviet Politics and Society (SPPS)

ISSN 1614-3515

Founded in 2004 and refereed since 2007, SPPS makes available affordable English-, German- and Russian-language studies on the history of the countries of the former Soviet bloc from the late Tsarist period to today. It publishes approximately 20 volumes per year, and focuses on issues in transitions to and from democracy such as economic crisis, identity formation, civil society development, and constitutional reform in CEE and the NIS. SPPS also aims to highlight so far understudied themes in East European studies such as right-wing radicalism, religious life, higher education, or human rights protection. The authors and titles of previously published and forthcoming manuscripts are listed at the end of this book. For a full description of the series and reviews of its books, see http://www.ibidem-verlag.de/red/spps.

Note for authors (as of 2007): After successful review, fully formatted and carefully edited electronic master copies of up to 250 pages will be published as b/w A5 paperbacks and marketed in Germany (e.g. vlb.de, buchkatalog.de, amazon.de). English-language books will, in addition, be marketed internationally (e.g. amazon.com). For longer books, formatting/editorial assistance, different binding, oversize maps, coloured illustrations and other special arrangements, authors' fees between €100 and €1500 apply. Publication of German doctoral dissertations follows a separate procedure. Authors are asked to provide a high-quality electronic picture on the object of their study for the book's front-cover. Younger authors may add a foreword from an established scholar. Monograph authors and collected volume editors receive two free as well as further copies for a reduced authors' price, and will be asked to contribute to marketing their book as well as finding reviewers and review journals for them. These conditions are subject to yearly review, and to be modified, in the future. Further details at www.ibidem-verlag.de/red/spps-authors.

Editorial correspondence & manuscripts should, until 2008, be sent to: Dr. Andreas Umland, DAAD, German Embassy, vul. Bohdana Khmelnitskoho 25, UA-01901 Kiev, Ukraine; umland@stanfordalumni.org.

Business correspondence & review copy requests should be sent to: *ibidem*-Verlag, Julius-Leber-Weg 11, D-30457 Hannover, Germany; tel.: +49(0)511-2622200; fax: +49(0)511-2622201; spps@ibidem-verlag.de.

Book orders & payments should be made via the publisher's electronic book shop at: http://www.ibidem-verlag.de/red/SPPS_EN/

Recent Volumes

72 *Christine Teichmann*
Die Hochschultransformation im heutigen Osteuropa
Kontinuität und Wandel bei der Entwicklung des postkommunistischen Universitätswesens
Mit einem Vorwort von Oskar Anweiler
ISBN 978-3-89821-842-9

73 *Julia Kusznir*
Der politische Einfluss von Wirtschaftseliten in russischen Regionen
Eine Analyse am Beispiel der Erdöl- und Erdgasindustrie, 1992-2005
Mit einem Vorwort von Wolfgang Eichwede
ISBN 978-3-89821-821-4

74 *Alena Vysotskaya*
Russland, Belarus und die EU-Osterweiterung
Zur Minderheitenfrage und zum Problem der Freizügigkeit des Personenverkehrs
Mit einem Vorwort von Katlijn Malfliet
ISBN 978-3-89821-822-1

75 *Heiko Pleines (Hrsg.)*
Corporate Governance in post-sozialistischen Volkswirtschaften
ISBN 978-3-89821-766-8

76 *Stefan Ihrig*
Wer sind die Moldawier?
Rumänismus versus Moldowanismus in Historiographie und Schulbüchern der Republik Moldova, 1991-2006
Mit einem Vorwort von Holm Sundhaussen
ISBN 978-3-89821-466-7

77 *Galina Kozhevnikova in collaboration with Alexander Verkhovsky and Eugene Veklerov*
Ultra-Nationalism and Hate Crimes in Contemporary Russia
The 2004-2006 Annual Reports of Moscow's SOVA Center
With a foreword by Stephen D. Shenfield
ISBN 978-3-89821-868-9

78 *Florian Küchler*
The Role of the European Union in Moldova's Transnistria Conflict
With a foreword by Christopher Hill
ISBN 978-3-89821-850-4

79 *Bernd Rechel*
The Long Way Back to Europe
Minority Protection in Bulgaria
With a foreword by Richard Crampton
ISBN 978-3-89821-863-4

To my parents, Barbara and Peter

Contents

List of Tables, Maps and Pictures

Tables

Maps

Pictures

List of Abbreviations

BYUT   *Blok: Yulia Tymoshenko (Block of Yulia Tymoshenko)*

KGB   *Komitet gosudarstvennoi bezopasnosti* (The Committee of State Security)

KPU   *Kommunistychna partiya Ukrayiny* (The Communist Party of Ukraine)

NKVD   *Narodnyi kommissariat vnutrennikh del* (The People's Commissariat of Internal Affairs)

OUN   *Orhanizatsiya Ukrayins'kykh Natsionalistiv* (Organisation of Ukrainian Nationalists)

SDPU-o   *Sotsial-demokratychna partiya Ukrayiny (ob'yednana)* (The Social-Democratic Party of Ukraine–united)

SPU   *Sotsialistychna partiya Ukrayiny* (The Socialist Party of Ukraine)

UNA   *Ukrayins'ka Narodna Respublika* (The Ukrainian People's Republic)

UPA   *Ukrayins'ka Povstans'ka Armiya* (Ukrainian Insurgent Army)

ZUNR   *Zakhidna Ukrains'ka Narodna Respublika* (West Ukrainian People's Republic)

ZYU   *Za Yedynu Ukrayinu* (For One Ukraine)

List of Appendices

Acknowledgements

I would like to express my gratitude to my PhD supervisor Dr. Kasia Wolczuk for her support and encouragement. My thanks also go to firstly the ESRC for the research studentship (R42200134405) as well as subsequently the Leverhulme Trust (SAS/2005/0055), both of whose generous financial support enabled this book to be realised. I am also indebted to the staff at CREES for their continued help, valuable ideas and suggestions. I am grateful to Marea and Tricia in the CREES office for their patient assistance.

This study would not have been possible without the assistance and support of many people in Ukraine. I thank you all; in particular, in Kiev, Andriy, Mykola, Masha, Larisa, Nikolaiy, Natasha, Yura and Maksim. Special thanks in Luhans'k to Sergei, Raisa, Olga and Sasha, Nina and Galina. In Kharkiv, many thanks to Volodymyr Kravchenko, Olga Fillipova, Sergei Viktorovich and Lena Vladimirovna. Thank you also to the many individuals who gave their time and thoughts during interviews and discussions.

I would like to thank my family and friends for their endless patience and support. In particular, thanks must go to John, Monty, Valya, Paul, Anton and Ariadna, Darroch, Jamie and Dave, Francois and Luda, John and Jo. Many thanks to my parents, Peter and Barbara for always being there.

Finally, I would like to thank the publishers of the journals below, who kindly gave me permission to print material, which has previously been published in the following articles:

"Understanding regionalism and the politics of identity in Ukraine's eastern borderlands", *Nationalities Papers*, 34, 2, May 2006: 157-174.

"Contestation and negotiation: Regionalism and the politics of school textbooks in Ukraine's eastern borderlands", *Nations and Nationalism*, 12, 4, October 2006: 681-697.

"(Re)inventing the Past: The Politics of 'National' History in the Ukrainian Classroom", *Studies in Ethnicity of Nationalism*, *Special Edition*, 6, 2, October 2006: 40-55.

"Compliance or contradiction? Teaching 'History' in the 'New' Ukraine. A View from Ukraine's Eastern Borderlands", *Europe-Asia Studies*, 59, 3, May 2007: 501-517.

Foreword

This book addresses a highly topical issue regarding the relationship of regional identities and an overarching national identity in contemporary Ukraine. This complex relationship is analysed in the book through the study of the teaching of Ukrainian history in Ukraine after the demise of the USSR and of the perception of the new historical narrative among teachers and schoolchildren in three *oblasts* of Eastern Ukraine.

The book argues for the importance of taking regional identities in Ukraine seriously. Demonstrating analytical skills and originality, it suggests that the focus on state-led nation-building often leads scholars underestimating the multiplicity of people's identities, particularly the significance of their regional identities. The author argues that many studies of the post-communist transition have overlooked the contribution to nation-building projects of 'ordinary people', who accept, reject or 'renegotiate' state-supported narratives. This book redresses this imbalance, providing a wealth of empirical evidence about varying responses from teachers and schoolchildren to new interpretations of Ukraine's history to be found in state-approved textbooks published in the last decade.

The author draws original conclusions about the formation of identities in Eastern Ukraine and convincingly shows that the wide-spread view that the people of Eastern Ukraine lack a sense of Ukrainian national identity is, in effect, erroneous. The author argues for Ukraine's unique form of regionalism, to be understood not in terms of divisions, but rather differences and diversity. Overall, this piece of research represents an original addition to our understanding of the complex and much discussed issue of identity change in contemporary Ukraine and provides an essential contribution to Ukrainian studies and more generally, post-Soviet studies.

Vera Tolz
University of Manchester
United Kingdom

Introduction

This study seeks to explore the processes of identity change, which have been occurring across Ukraine in the post-1991 period. Rather than seeing national identity as something given, preordained or constant, the study respects the fluidity, dynamism and ever-evolving nature of national identities. A multidimensional approach is utilised which explores ways that national identity is not only (re)constructed by the Ukrainian state, but also how it is contested and negotiated at a variety of different levels by different actors.

The Research Gap

Regarding the issues of national identity and identity change, both Ukrainian and Western academics have undertaken much research concerning Ukraine, particularly in the post-Soviet period. However, whilst much of the results of this body of thought are illuminating and have enhanced our understanding of the issues, nevertheless there are shortcomings and 'gaps' which this study seeks to address. Much research has concentrated on the role of ethnicity and language use as the chief determinants in defining self-identification in Ukraine. This has been to the expense of a thorough evaluation of the role of the region in individuals' self-identification processes. There needs to be a better understanding of not just the role of such determinants in isolation, but a further engagement into how contours such as ethnicity, language use and region interact, crosscut and reinforce each other in a whole myriad of ways across Ukraine.

This study takes a **'regional'** approach to examine identity change across Ukraine. Much academic attention during the post-1991 period has been applied to the so-called 'west-east' divide across Ukraine. This research seeks to uncover and unpack such conceptualisations, choosing to further understanding of the meta-region of 'Eastern Ukraine'. A comparative approach is taken, in which three areas, adjacent to the Russian-Ukrainian state border are chosen for the location of empirical research. In these areas 'mixed' Russian-Ukrainian identities exist today, resulting from the erosion of linguistic and cultural boundaries between Russians and Ukrainians under Tsarist and more particularly Soviet 'russification' policies.[1] Such identities with a lack of historical consciousness and a weak sense of difference from Russia present a great challenge to the Ukrainian state.

Whilst the Ukrainian state has many different 'tools' through which it can aim to (re)construct national identity across Ukraine, this study concentrates on how identity change has been occurring in the realm of education.[2] It explores whether and how the state has used this 'tool' to achieve its goal of a unified Ukrainian identity and in particular reformulating the interpretation of historical relations with Russia. It also examines to what extent central policies have been adopted or adapted at the local state level. It takes into account how national identity is constructed. Further, it looks not only at official rhetoric and policy but also at its subsequent implementation. Thus, this research is innovative, while recognising the importance of 'top-down' processes for identity construction, in particular the role of the state, propagated by existing models, it examines such processes as part of a wider interaction between 'top-down' and 'bottom-up' processes.[3] This responds to calls to understand how popular notions of identity are produced through, against and within state discourse.[4] The Soviet practice of fixed attribution of 'passport ethnicity' failed and still fails today to capture the enormous degree of flexibility and identity in terms of both language and ethnic identities in

---

1   Pirie, P.S., "National Identity and Politics in Southern and Eastern Ukraine", *Europe-Asia Studies*, 48, 7, 1996: 1079-1104.

2   For a thorough overview of the use of education as a tool of the state see, Bourdieu, P., "Rethinking the State: Genesis and Structure of the Bureaucratic Field", *Sociological Theory*, 12, 1, 1994:18.

3   Brubaker, R., "Nationhood and the National Question in the Soviet Union and Post-Soviet Eurasia: An Institutionalist Account", *Theory and Society* 23, 1, 47-78; Breuilly, J., *Nationalism and the State*, Manchester: Manchester University Press, 1993: 7.

4   Jackson, L., "Identity, Language, and Transformation in Eastern Ukraine: A Case Study of Zaporizhzhia", in Kuzio, T., *Contemporary Ukraine: Dynamics of Post-Soviet Transformation*, Armonk, NY: M.E.Sharpe, 1998: 99-113.

areas such as the Russian-Ukrainian borderlands.[5] Thus, this research responds to calls for an understanding of the multi-layered, dynamic, and ever changing nature of identity particularly in the context of the vast political and societal transformations taking place in post-Soviet societies.[6] In terms of methodology, this study is based mainly on qualitative research methods. Much research has been conducted across the post-Soviet world in general and Ukraine in particular using large-scale opinion polls and surveys.[7] The results of such work have provided a clearer general picture of changes taking place. However, there is a clear need for more in-depth qualitative research at the micro level which can provide a greater understanding of the nuances within wider societal processes.

Research questions

Empirical research was undertaken to examine how individuals subjectively attempt to answer three overarching questions. Regarding the first question, *'Where are we from?'* the study has investigated how 'historical' identities are affecting wider national identities across Ukraine at a variety of different levels by different actors. The second question, *'Where are we?'* has necessitated a thorough examination of the importance of the 'regional' factor within processes of identity change across Ukraine. The study chose to undertake empirical research in three study areas in Ukraine's eastern borderlands, in order to gain a picture of how individuals view the importance of spatial politics across Ukraine. Finally, the third question, *'Who we are not?'* seeks to explore to what extent Russia is perceived as Ukraine's real 'other' in the politics of identity. Whilst these three questions provide an overarching framework for the study, more specific research questions are outlined below.

---

5   Chizhikova, L., "Russko-ukrainskoe pogranich'e: istoriia i sud'by traditsionno-bytovoi kul'tury (XIX-XX vv.)", Moscow: *Nauka*, 1988: 14-69.

6   Miller, A.H., Klobucar, T.F., Reisinger, W.M. and Hesli, V.L., "Social Identities in Russia, Ukraine, and Lithuania", *Post-Soviet Affairs* 14, 1998: 248-286.

7   Arel, D. and Wilson, A., "The Ukrainian parliamentary elections", *RFE/RL Research Report*, 3, 26, 1994: 6-17.

What kind of nation-building policies have the central authorities intro-duced in education?

Focus here is on the field of history, exploring to what degree a revised, Ukrainian historical narrative has evolved in school textbooks across Ukraine since 1991. This textbook analysis examines not only key events in Ukraine's history, but also to what degree Russia is represented as an 'other'.

How are these centrally constructed narratives received at the regional and local levels in the three chosen study areas in the eastern border-lands of Ukraine?

This section involves the reception of the state narrative at a variety of different local scales. Firstly, there is a thorough analysis of regional history and geography textbooks utilised in schools in the three study areas. The focus here is to assess to what extent such regional narratives seek to accelerate or dilute central state narratives or even to reject them. Secondly, the role of school history teachers in this process is explored, questioning whether they are simply the passive 'transmitters' of information or whether they actively negotiate and contest the state narrative.   Finally, the study examines how schoolchildren in the three study areas have negotiated the state historical narrative?

What importance is attached to the 'region' in the three study areas?

Here, the study seeks to understand how both schoolteachers and schoolchildren perceive the spatial politics of Ukraine, studying the impor-tance of their 'region'. Attention focuses on perceived differences between 'eastern' and 'western' Ukraine and also to what degree is Russia seen as an 'other', a foreign country, by analysing opinions concerning the Rus-sian/Ukrainian state border.

Book Structure

Chapter 1 'maps' identities in Ukraine, arguing that while academic de-bate has focused on the importance of ethnic and linguistic differences across Ukraine, such assumptions have been misplaced. Instead, the chapter posits a thorough engagement with the 'regional' differences across Ukraine, and their effects on the state's nation-building policies.

Chapter 2 examines the significance of regional diversity across Ukraine. It is argued that owing to the diversity of historical legacies of many regions of modern-day Ukraine, regionalism is a far more complex phenomenon than a simple, dichotomous 'west versus east' divide. The inherent peculiarity of the Ukrainian version of regionalism is not that it represents a danger of imminent state disintegration in the face of secessionist claims or a split along the River *Dnipro*, but rather the challenge it presents in creating an all-embracing modern, civic Ukrainian national identity. In an attempt to move beyond the standardised perception of Ukraine, neatly divided between 'west' and 'east', the chapter takes as a point of departure an eight-region framework, which was further modified by the author to create a framework of ten regions. Furthermore, to illuminate the inherent nuances and subtleties within and between regions in Ukraine, this chapter deconstructs the concept of 'Eastern Ukraine' as a unitary, homogenous space, assessing how it relates to the ten-region model. Three oblasts, all situated adjacent to the Ukrainian-Russian border, are chosen as ideal 'sites' for the focus of the study.

Chapter 3 assesses how history textbooks are utilised by the state as 'tools' to introduce school children to key historical episodes around which a modern Ukrainian national identity can be moulded. The study examines to what extent, since 1991 has there been a crystallisation of a single, state-sponsored, historical narrative in Ukraine. Secondly, the study assesses to what degree Russia is presented as a distinct 'other'. Finally, the chapter assesses to what degree there has been a standardisation of history textbooks used in schools across the whole of Ukraine or to what extent regional variations have continued to exist across the country.

Chapter 4 focuses on 'ordinary people's' perceptions of Ukraine's past, examining how this state-sponsored historical narrative is actually *negotiated and contested at the local level*. The results of qualitative in-depth interviews with school directors, history teachers and schoolchildren are used to examine to what extent the central message of the history textbooks is clearly transferred or whether any dilution, contradictions or open avoidance of certain issues is occurring. More research continues with an analysis of group interviews with school children. Attention is placed upon how the historical narrative is 'perceived' and to what extent such perceptions coincide with the content of the historical narrative.

Chapter 5 focuses attention on the importance of the regional factor in Ukraine's identity politics and secondly that of Russia as Ukraine's 'other'. The chapter assesses regional historical narratives, exploring how they complement or contradict the state's 'official' narrative. This is achieved by a content analysis of various 'regional' geography and history textbooks. In such a fashion, the extent can be gauged of how the view of education elites in the regions actually corresponds to the 'official' view of Ukraine's history, laid out by the centre in Kiev. Secondly, empirical data generated during fieldwork in the study areas is utilised to examine how individuals reflect on the importance of the 'region' in Ukraine today and also to what extent Russia is perceived as the 'other' in the identity politics of Ukraine.

Chapter 6 attempts to draw together the various strands of this study and make some concluding remarks.

Methodological issues

Empirical data was generated during time spent in the three study areas in Ukraine in 2003, from both primary and secondary sources. Primary sources included ethnographic interviews undertaken at schools and universities in each of the three study areas involved education officials, school directors, school history teachers and schoolchildren. Secondary sources included the analysis of official documents, newspaper articles, social surveys and opinion polls, and other published research undertaken by both Ukrainian and western academics, together with content analysis of history textbooks.

A qualitative approach

Most of the methods used in this research were *qualitative* in nature. Qualitative research can be defined as an attempt to present the social world, and perspectives on that world, in terms of concepts, behaviours, perceptions and accounts of the people it is about.

Qualitative methods were chosen for this research project as they provide a depth and a richness, which fails often to be highlighted in many quantitative studies. Concerning academic research in the post-Soviet space, qualitative research methods are particularly useful as they permit the researcher to remain flexible in a rapidly changing environment, also not being forced to stay within the bounds of questions and categories, constructed before the fieldwork, in a different cultural environment. Many opinion polls and surveys have been carried out, with their results shedding light on many interesting trends at the macro level. However, such studies often fail to capture some of the subtleties within the wider processes and test the theoretical assumptions upon which they were based.[8]

The aim of this project was to examine the construction and negotiation of national identity in Ukraine. Qualitative methods allow individuals themselves to express how they feel about a certain issue and how it impacts on their daily lives, rather than being forced into choosing from categories, provided by the interviewer. Thus they provide an ideal way to assess the *meanings* and *perceptions* people place on notions of identity.

A *case study approach* was utilised in this research. Three case study areas were chosen in Ukraine, namely the oblast capitals, Luhans'k, Kharkiv and Sumy. These places are all situated in Ukraine's eastern borderlands adjacent to the Russian border. As such, they provide a spatial dimension for comparative research assessing how identity change is occurring in Ukraine. The case study approach facilitates the study of identity change to take place at both the micro and macro levels, and between them, focusing our attention on how identities are constructed and contested at a variety of different levels by a number of individual actors. This method generates the empirical findings of micro-level research to inform the wider theoretical understandings of the politics of identity in Ukraine.[9]

Choice of methods

The methods used in this research project included; in-depth expert interviews, group interviews with schoolchildren and content analysis. All the interviews were taped and later transcribed.

---

8   Pilkington, H., *Russia's youth and its culture*, London: Routledge, 1994.
9   Burawoy, M. et al., *Ethnography Unbound*, Berkeley: University of California Press, 1991: 10-11.

Expert interviews

Interviews were conducted with a range of experts in 2003 in the cities of Kiev, Luhans'k, Kharkiv and Sumy. These experts included academics, regional education officials, school history teachers and school directors. The interviews were semi-structured: with academics, they focused on wide ranging issues involving regionalism and national identity in Ukraine. With other experts, interviews focused on the changes taking place in the Ukrainian education system; the new Ukrainian history textbooks and how they differed from the previous Soviet textbooks; the representation of specific periods of Ukraine's history; issues surrounding regionalism in Ukraine; opinions concerning Ukraine's relationship with Russia and the Ukrainian-Russian state border.

Group interviews

Group interviews took place in the three study areas in 2003, ten to twenty schoolchildren in each interview. Schoolchildren in Grades 10 and 11 of the Ukrainian education system (fifteen to seventeen year olds) were chosen for several reasons. Firstly, from a practical point of view, these groups of fifteen to seventeen year olds were finishing their school years and also their formal and compulsory historical education. Thus, data generated from this group could indicate how the 'official' historical narrative was being negotiated at the micro level. Secondly, as previous ethnological studies have highlighted, whilst individual understandings of self-identification occur in certain stages, at this age an individual takes on a deeper awareness of their national consciousness.[10] Thirdly, this age group has grown up in a period of rapid social, economic, cultural and political transformations in Ukraine. They were born in the Soviet Union, yet are the first generation of children to have been totally schooled in independent Ukraine. Thus, it will be extremely interesting to examine to what extent these children's reflections on Ukraine's

---

10   Snezhkova, I.A., "K probleme izuchenia etnicheskogo samosoznani u detei i iunoshestva", *Sovetskaya etnografia*, 1982, 1, quoted in, Filippova, O., "Ukrainians and Russians in Eastern Ukraine: Ethnic Identity and Citizenship in the Light of Ukrainian Nation-Building, http://www.unl.ac.uk/ukrainecentre/WP/12.html, accessed 8 October 2001.

past coincide or differ not only from the new 'official' state narrative, but also from their parents' generation's views.

In each of the study areas, interviews were conducted at five secondary schools. For the interviews, the author had in advance agreed with teachers in each individual school for a group of ten to twenty children from Grades 10 and 11 to be assembled for a group interview. It should be noted that these groups of children were taught by the teachers, who were also interviewed as part of the research process.

Content analysis

A thorough analysis of the content of textbooks used in Ukraine's 'History of Ukraine' course was undertaken. The results are outlined in Chapter 3. Also various regional textbooks, in each study area, used in the 'History of the native region' or 'Geography of the native region' were analysed with the results highlighted in Chapter 5.

1 Mapping Identities in Ukraine

...[N]ations living in this region lacked what was naturally, clearly precisely and con-
cretely present in everyday life and community consciousness of nations in Western
Europe: A reality in their own national and state framework, a capital city, a har-
mony between economy and politics, a unified social elite etc...In Eastern
Europe...a national framework was something that had to be created, repaired,
fought for and constantly protected, not only against the power factors existing in
the dynastic state, but also from the indifference exhibited by a certain proportion of
the country's own inhabitants, as well as the wavering state of national consciousness.[11]

The demise of the Soviet Union, coupled with the rise of the nation-
state being seen as the ultimate expression of the 'right for national self-
determination', led to the post-Soviet states commencing processes of
redefining their relations with their neighbours and simultaneously forging an
internal coherent 'body politic' out of often highly diversified populations. In
Ukraine, these processes have been far from straightforward. Ukraine is not a
nation-state in the classical understanding of the term, yet it is not unique in
this respect.[12] Its peculiarity lies not in the fact that there are sizeable national
minorities within her citizenry, but more in the fact that the ethnic Ukrainian
titular majority does not constitute a unified, homogenous and coherent
nation. Modern day Ukraine is a state riddled with competing and contradict-
ing patterns of ethnic, linguistic, religious and regional diversity. This is a
result of the historical legacies of various regions of today's Ukraine being
part of the Polish-Lithuanian Commonwealth, Habsburg, Ottoman, Tsarist

---

11   Bibo, I., "The Distress of the East European Small States", in Nagy, K., (ed.),
      Democracy, Revolution and Self-Determination: Selected Writings of Istvan Bibo,
      Boulder, CO: Social Science Monographs, 1991.
12   The nation-state is defined here as "an ideal where all self-governing units – states
      – correspond with cultural distinctive units – nations". See McCrone, D., *The Soci-
      ology of Nationalism*, London: Routledge, 1998: 9. The author draws the reader's
      attention to the fact that most states are not nation-states, but 'present' themselves
      as such.

and Soviet Empires. As such, what it means to be 'Ukrainian' and what are the chief determinants of a Ukrainian national identity vary across the country. Such cleavages have inevitably made the task of the Ukrainian state of creating a unified Ukrainian national identity based on an understanding of who 'we' are and who 'we are not' extremely tenuous yet nevertheless urgent.

This chapter assesses the significance of these societal divisions in an attempt to distinguish what is the chief determinant of national identity in Ukraine. It is argued that while academic debate has focused on the assumed importance of ethnicity and language as markers of identity, such attention may have been misplaced. The chapter posits the need for a thorough examination of regional cleavages across Ukraine. As a result of the afore-mentioned diverse historical experiences of different regions of Ukraine, one's place of residence acts as the key determinant in national identity, crosscut-ting, rather than reinforcing other cleavages such as ethnicity and language.

1.1   Ukrainian/Russian nexus

Ukraine's 'national question' has often been portrayed in the context of a titular ethnic majority (Ukrainian) and large numbers of national minorities, of which Russians form by far the largest number. The results of the 2001 census show that Ukrainians comprise 77.8 percent (37.7 million) of the population, with Russians making up 17.3 percent (8.3 million).[13] The other main ethnic groups in Ukraine are Jews, Belarussians, Moldovans, Crimean Tatars, Bulgarians, Poles, Hungarians, Romanians and other small groups (all of which claim less than 1 percent of the population). These figures are indeed highly significant when compared with the figures from the 1989 census. Over this twelve-year period, whilst there has been negligible migration of ethnic Russians back to Russia, overall three million ethnic Russians have seemingly 'disappeared', or in fact, by 2001, come to define

---

13   The census was conducted in December 2001 with the data being released by the State Committee of Statistics of Ukraine in early 2003. In comparison, from the 1989 census, Ukrainians comprised 72 percent of the population and Russians 22.1 percent, see Ministry of Statistics of the USSR, "Natsional'nyi sostav naseleniya

themselves as Ukrainians. This is evidence of the fluidity of identities in Ukraine and the difficulties encompassed when forcing individuals into choosing between two separate categories of 'Ukrainian' or 'Russian' in a national census, when in reality, for many people, these two categories are more blurred, with no clear lines of distinction.

As a result of the fact that Ukrainians and Russians are by far the most numerous ethnic groups in Ukraine, comprising over 95 percent of the population, much attention has been paid to this nexus. In particular, during Ukraine's early years of independence, commentators assumed that Ukraine's large 'Russian minority' would not accept Ukraine as a sovereign state and thus severely hamper the nation-building projects of the Ukrainian state. For example, in 1994, a US intelligence community's assessment of Ukraine found that there were grave dangers that the large Russian national minority might secede or put a great deal of pressure on Kiev to re-enter a union with Russia.[14] However, in many respects Russians have been misconceived as representing a classical 'national minority' and a 'diaspora'. Clifford defines a diaspora as characterised by a group experiencing a "shared, ongoing history of displacement."[15] Similarly, Safran also attempts to define diasporas as "Expatriate minority communities...that maintain a memory, vision, or myth about their original homeland...that see the ancestral home as a place of eventual return...(and whose) consciousness and solidarity are importantly defined by this continuous relationship with the homeland."[16] Yet, many Russians, especially in the southern and eastern regions, argue that Russians have lived in Ukraine for centuries and therefore form a legitimate part of Ukraine's land and history. From this, comes the

---

SSSR po rezultatam vsesouznoj perepisi naselenia 1989", Moscow: *Finansy i Sta-tistika*, 1991.

14   Williams, D. and Smith, R.J., "Dire U.S Forecast for Ukraine Conflict", *International Herald Tribune*, 26 January, 1994.

15   Clifford, J., "Diasporas", *Cultural Anthropology*, 9, 3, 1994: 306.

16   Safran, W., "Diasporas in modern societies: Myths of Homeland and Return", *Diaspora: A Journal of Transnational Studies*, 1, 1, 1991: 8.

group's dislike of being classified as a 'national minority', or as a 'diaspora', as they claim to be in fact, 'indigenous'.[17]

To fully understand the Russian/Ukrainian identity nexus in Ukraine, one must take into account the legacies of Soviet nationality policy. In the Soviet Union, nationality was defined ascriptively, with a strong bias towards either one's father's nationality or to the republic of residence.[18] This official practice of privileging blood ancestry over actual cultural/social practices and self-identification, allied to the official policy of 'national in form, socialist in content', served to undermine the meaning of nationality. In Ukraine, this is especially the case where the rates of intermarriage between Russians and Ukrainians were extremely high.[19] As such, census figures do not offer an adequate method to understand the contradictory and complex nature of national identities in Soviet Ukraine, in particular in its southern and eastern regions. The results of ethnographic research in the Ukrainian-Russian bi-cultural belt clearly demonstrate this with several respondents describing their ethnicity as "under one regime, we were Ukrainians, under another we were Russians, but frankly speaking we do not know who we are."[20]

In independent Ukraine, surveys have highlighted the fact that the leg-acy of Soviet nationality practice remains. A survey, undertaken in December 1997, found that 69 percent of respondents viewed themselves as Ukraini-ans, 20 percent as Russians and 6 percent as 'Ukrainian and Russian', results similar to the 1989 findings.[21] However, when in the same survey, respondents were given the opportunity to see their identities in more situational or dualistic terms, the results were very different; 56 percent saw

---

17   Szporluk, R., "Russians in Ukraine and Problems of Ukrainian Identity in the USSR", in Potichny, P.J., (ed.), *Ukraine in the 1970s*, Oakville, Ontario: Mosaic, 1975: 196.

18   For thorough examinations of the Soviet nationality policy and its legacies, see, Simonsen, S.V., "Inheriting the Soviet policy toolbox: Russia's dilemma over ascrip-tive nationality", *Europe-Asia Studies*, 51, 6, 1999: 1069-87.

19   See Silver, B., "The ethnic and language dimensions in Russian and Soviet censuses", in Clem, R, (ed.), *Research Guide to the Russian and Soviet Censuses*, Ithaca: Cornell University Press, 70-97.

20   Chizhykova, L.N., "Russkoe-Ukrainskoe pogranich'e: istoriia i sud'by traditsionno-bytovoi kul'tury (XIX-XX vv.)", Moscow: *Nauka*, 1988:14-69.

21   Pogrebinskii, M., (ed.), "Politicheskie nastroeniia nakanune vyborov", Ukraina, 1997, Kiev: Centre for Political Research and Conflictology, 1997.

themselves as Ukrainians, 11 percent Russians and 27 percent as both Ukrainian and Russian. This mixed/dual identity was heavily concentrated in the urban areas of southeastern Ukraine, accounting for 51 percent in the Donbas region (Luhans'k and Donets'k) and 43 percent in Kharkiv, Dnipropet-rovsk and Zaporizhzhia.[22]

To understand the origins of such mixed identities, Ukraine's role in the Soviet Union needs to be addressed. Despite the fact that Ukraine developed rapidly under Soviet rule, modernisation, in its Soviet version, did not create an 'imagined community'.[23] As a result of Soviet policies, particularly in the areas of culture, history and language, Ukrainian national identity was weakened and increasingly submerged into an all-embracing 'Soviet' identity. In the area of historiography, from the 1930s the official Soviet version of historical events shifted to a schemata of history which integrated much of the old Russian imperial 'statist' historical narrative into a dogmatic Marxist methodology, ready to legitimate the current political demands and realities of the Soviet state. History was used to serve the policy of unifying non-Russian peoples around the Russian 'elder brother'. In 1947 and 1954 new policies in historical education codified the eastern Slavs as historically being part of one *Russk narod* (Russian people).[24] The East Slavic peoples were propagated as having common origins in the proto-state of Kiev Rus'. From then on, political alliance between the Eastern Slavs was deemed natural. Soviet historiography portrayed the Pereiaslav Agreement in 1648 between the Ukrainian Cossacks and the Tsarist authorities as the natural culmination of a desire by the Ukrainians to reunite with their Russian brothers.[25]

Any challenges to this scheme of historiography were banned, which became the fate of the work of the Ukrainian historian Mykhailo Hrushevskyi. In his *Istoriya Ukrayiny-Rusi* (History of Ukraine-Rus) Hrushevskyi provided a counter-claim to the traditional Russian views concerning the origins of the

---

22   *Ibid.*
23   For a thorough overview of modernisation and how it can be applied to Ukraine, see, Krawchenko, B., *Social Change and National Consciousness in Twentieth Century Ukraine*, Basingstoke and London: Macmillan, 1985.
24   Velychenko, S., "The Official Soviet View of Ukrainian History", *Journal of Ukrainian Studies*, 10, 2, 1985: 84.
25   Morrison, J., "Pereyeslav and after: the Russian-Ukrainian Relationship", *International Affairs*, 69, 4, 1993: 677-703.

east Slavic peoples arguing that Ukraine was a direct and sole successor to the medieval state of Kiev Rus'. This 'statist' approach saw the Galycian-Volynian princedom and the Cossack state of the seventeenth and eighteenth centuries as embodiments of Ukrainian statehood.[26] Such ideas had been adopted by Ukrainian national elites at the time of the Ukrainian Revolution and in the following period of *natsionalne vidrodzhennya* (national regeneration) under the Soviets in the late 1920s. However, the period was short-lived, leaving the project of promulgating the 'national idea' across Ukraine incomplete. Instead, from the 1930s, the Soviet authorities stated that the Soviet Union was following a unique modernisation path with the end result being a 'socialist commonwealth'. It was asserted that ethnic differences would decline as a result of intermarriage and assimilation processes, with the result being the "steady convergence of all nations and peoples of the Soviet Union, and the molding of a new, historical community, the Soviet people."[27]

The interaction of such processes in the realm of history, together with the erosion of linguistic and cultural boundaries between Russians and Ukrainians, led many people to hold mixed identities, despite the fact that formally, as recorded on their passports, their 'official' nationality may have been 'Ukrainian' or 'Russian'. Thus, it is worth noting that in the USSR, Russians were as strongly influenced by local Ukrainian culture as Ukrainians were by Russian culture. In particular, territorial identities were promoted not only to the expense of Ukrainian national identity, but also to Russian ethnic and national identities. For example, it is often argued that Russians in Ukraine are different from the *moskali* (muscovites), a derogatory term used by Ukrainians for Russians in general. Instead, Russians "have taken on certain local values and attitudes, which have created clear differences between them and the Russians in Russia."[28] This, together with the eco-

---

26   For an overview of Hrushevskyi's work and its influence on the Ukrainian national movement, see Prymak, T., *Mykhailo Hrushevsky: The Politics of National Culture*, Toronto: University of Toronto Press, 1987.

27   For a classic statement of this ideology, see Bromlei, I., (ed.), "Present-day Ethnic Processes in the USSR", *Progress*, Moscow, 1982: 414-452.

28   Hrytsak, Y., "Ukraina, 1991-1995rr: nova politychna natsiia", *Skhid*, 4, 1996: 15.

nomic factor, has been used to explain why large numbers of ethnic Russians voted for Ukrainian independence in December 1991.[29]

The prevalence of such fluid and competing identities in Ukraine has meant that there have been extremely low levels of political support for parties advocating the 'Russian idea' except in Crimea. For example, the Russophile Party, which advocated an economic union of Ukraine and Russia, the status of the Russian language in Ukraine to be upgraded to the level of a second state language and rejected attempts to legalise the 'political division of one people' was unsuccessful, in the 1998 parliamentary elections, gaining only 0.9 percent of the vote.[30] Similarly the Union Party, which supported Ukraine entering into an "inter-state union" with Russia and Belarus, gained 0.7 percent of the vote.[31] Also it argued that "nationalist ideology [that is] forced upon society" was one of the chief reasons for the desperate situation in Ukraine and again called for the legalisation of Russian as a second state language.

Similarly in the 2002 parliamentary elections, the explicitly pro-Russian party, *Rus'kyi blok* (Russian bloc), gained over 4 percent of the vote only in Crimea (4.76 percent) and the City of Sevastopol (8.83 percent).[32] Instead, Russians have tended to vote for left wing parties such as the Communist Party of Ukraine (KPU), which has called for greater links between Russia and Ukraine, utilising ideas of 'pan-Slavism' and 'East Slavic Unity'. In Crimea and in the eastern and southern regions of Ukraine where the majority of Russians reside, there was strong support for the KPU. In Luhans'k region, KPU polled the highest percentage with 39.7 percent, whilst in Crimea it polled 33.9 percent. In Donets'k, Kharkiv, Dnipropetrovsk, Zaporizhzhia,

---

29   Nemyria, G., "Regionalism: An Underestimated Dimension of State-Building", in Wolchik, S.L. and Zviglyanich, V., *Ukraine: The Search for a National Identity*, Lanham, MA: Rowman and Littlefield, 2000, 183-198.

30   Wilson, A., *The Ukrainians: unexpected nation*, New Haven: Yale University Press, 2000, 216.

31   For the full results of the 1998 parliamentary elections, see *Holos Ukrayiny*, 8 April 1998, quoted in Solchanyk, R., *Ukraine and Russia: The Post-Soviet Transition*, Lanham, MA: Rowman and Littlefield, 2001, 143.

32   For a statistical breakdown of the results by regions, see www.cvk.ukrpack.net, accessed 15 April 2005.

Kherson and Mykolaiv, the figures were approximately 30 percent.[33] Such findings clearly demonstrate that Ukraine's internal diversity is far more complex than a simplistic Russian-Ukrainian ethnic divide.

1.2 Language: a marker of identity?

The lack of importance attached to a distinct 'ethnic' marker in identity issues in Ukraine led many commentators to forward a notion that to fully understand societal divisions and issues of identity across Ukraine, language use must be examined. For example, Arel has argued that the "private use of language is closer to the issue of [national] identity" than any other group indicator.[34] It is purported that Ukrainian society can be split into three groups, Ukrainophone Ukrainians, Russophone Russians and Russophone Ukrainians.

The debate over the actual numbers of Russian and Ukrainian speakers has been a subject hotly disputed. From the 1989 census figures, it is shown that 12.3 percent of ethnic Ukrainians perceive Russian to be their *ridna mova* (native tongue in Ukrainian) or *rodnoi yazyk* (in Russian).[35] However, such figures must be treated with a degree of caution. The census idea of 'native tongue' is highly ambiguous. It can be interpreted to mean the language of one's ancestors, the language one learnt in childhood or the language one is comfortable in at the present moment. As a result of the processes of russification, the language chosen for each category may well be different.[36]

---

33   It is not argued that support for the KPU is solely based on its 'East-Slavic Unity' ideas. Policies of social welfare may also prove attractive to voters in regions of Ukraine, undergoing vast economic transformations.For a statistical breakdown of the results by region, see www.cvk.ukrpack.net, accessed 15 April 2005.

34   Arel, D., "The Temptation of the Nationalising State", in Tismaneanu, V., (ed.), *Political Culture and Civil Society in Russia and the New States of Eurasia*, Armonk, N.Y: Sharpe, 1995:169.

35   Kaiser, R., *The Geography of Nationalism in Russia and the USSR*, Princeton: Princeton University Press, 273.

36   See Khmelko, V. and Arel, D., "The Russian Factor and Territorial Polarisation in Ukraine", *Harriman Review*, 9, 1-2, Spring 1996: 81-91.

This has led to recent studies looking at the *language of preference*, meaning the language that an individual will most commonly choose to use in everyday circumstance. Here, the results are rather different with the Ukrainophone Ukrainians comprising approximately 40-45 percent of the population, Russophone Russians 20-22 percent, Russophone Ukrainians 30-35 percent and Ukrainophone Russians a mere 1-3 percent.[37] Such figures denote that a minority speaks Ukrainian across Ukraine. Whilst in rural areas, Ukrainophones still predominate, in urban areas, they are an outright minority, continually being compelled to defend their rights *vis-à-vis* the dominant Russophone groups.[38] Here also, major regional differences in language practice were found. Surveys conducted between 1991-1994 found that whilst 77 percent of the population of 'west Ukraine' use Ukrainian as the language of preference, only 18.5 percent of the population of 'east Ukraine' do so.[39] In the capital, Kiev, where 72 percent of the city's population is Ukrainian (Soviet census), only 23.6 percent use Ukrainian as the language of preference.[40] However Ryabchuk argues that the *language of preference* like the *native language* category does not explain fully the complexities of language use in Ukraine. It is argued that nearly a third of Ukraine's population constantly move in and out of using Ukrainian and Russian owing to *circumstance* and their surroundings.[41] Ryabchuk therefore states the *language of preference* methodology hides the real language use as many Ukrainophone Ukrainians, in the semi-formal situation of an interview, may feel it best to reply in Russian, and thus give an artificially high figure for Russophone Ukrainians.[42]

Other studies argue that the ethnolinguistic divides across Ukraine are highly important in explaining the population's socio-political orientations and Ukraine's relations with Russia.[43] Furthermore, it was argued that the results of the 1994 presidential elections showed that support for the two key

---

37   Pogrebinskii, M., (ed.), "Politicheskie nastroeniia nakanune vyborov", 17.
38   Ryabchuk, M., "Civil Society and Nation Building in Ukraine", in Kuzio, T., (ed.), *Contemporary Ukraine: Dynamics of Post-Soviet Transformation*, Armonk: M.E. Sharpe, 1998: 89.
39   Arel, D. and Khmelko, V., "The Russian Factor and Terriotorial Polarisation", 81.
40   Arel, D., "Ukraine: The Temptation of the Nationalising State 170.
41   Ryabchuk, M., "Civil Society and Nation Building in Ukraine", 96.
42   *Ibid.*, 89.
43   Arel, D. and Khmelko, V., "The Russian Factor and Territorial Polarization", 81-91.

candidates split according to linguistic lines. This led to Kuchma gaining power, with the support of the densely populated and heavily russified regions of southeastern Ukraine.[44] Such an analysis fitted well with the alarmist scenarios of deep national cleavages in Ukraine, which were said to inevitably lead to Ukraine splitting into an 'east' and 'west' along linguistic lines.[45] Suffice it to say such commentaries fail to delineate where the country would be split, failing to take into account that divisions in Ukraine are not always overlapping, and also that there is a graduation and merging of differences, rather than one divide in Ukrainian society.[46] The great difficulties in assessing language use in Ukraine highlight the fact that the three competing ethnolinguistic groups cannot be seen to be separate and distinct groups as there is a great deal of crossover between them. In place of any concrete linguistic boundaries, individuals continually move in and out of the two languages depending on circumstances and on occasions, or at all times, use *surzhyk*, the hybrid Russian/Ukrainian mixture.[47] Such difficulties in assessing language use have led to a strong critique of the importance given to language in determining national identity in Ukraine. It is argued that language is important but not the over-riding and all-embracing factor in national identity. Connor argues that language use has never been a key issue in Ukrainian politics, stating:

> Would not the Ukrainian nation...be likely to persist even if the language were totally replaced by Russian, just as the Irish nation has persisted after the virtual dis-

---

44   See Arel, D. and Wilson, A., "Ukraine: Back to Eurasia?", *RFE/RL Research Report*, 5, 32, 19 August 1994.

45   "Ukraine: The Birth and Possible Death of a Country", *The Economist*, 7 May 1994.

46   Garnett, S.W., *Keystone in the Arch: Ukraine in the Emerging Security Architecture of Central and Eastern Europe*, Washington DC: Carnegie Endowment for International Peace, 1997: 8-21.

47   For more detailed discussions of the phenomenon of *surzhyk*, see Flier, M.S., "Surzhyk: The Rules of Engagement", in Gitelman, Z., Hajda, L., Himka, J-P. and Solchanyk, R., *Cultures and Nations of Central and Eastern Europe, Essays in Honor of Roman Szporluk, Harvard Ukrainian Studies*, vol. XXII, 1998; and Bilaniuk, L., "Speaking of Surzhyk: Ideologies and Mixed Languages", *Harvard Ukrainian Studies*, vol.XXI, nos.1-2, June 1997: 93-118.

appearance of Gaelic, despite 1920s slogans that described Gaelic and Irish identity as inseparable.[48]

Furthermore, a study published in 2002 using the results of surveys based on attitudes towards Russia provocatively argues that a Ukrainian nation building policy, concentrating on narrowing ethnic and linguistic divides throughout Ukraine, may prove extremely divisive and ultimately self-defeating.[49] Instead Shulman argues that if the goal of the state-led projects is to create political consensus, then the Ukrainian state should advocate the establishment of an 'East-Slavic' identity, which emphasises not the distinctions, but the closeness of Ukrainians and Russians.

1.3   A regional approach?

With the assumed importance attached to ethnic and linguistic markers seemingly misplaced and often exaggerated, the importance of other factors such as region of residence and socio-economic standing have been increasingly investigated. Pirie in a study of southern and eastern Ukraine found that many respondents held shifting or multiple national identities.[50] Categories such as 'Russian' or 'Ukrainian' were found to be over simplifications of a complex reality in which historic and demographic factors as well as language use and ethnicity were highly relevant in understanding forms of self-identification. Pirie's work was extremely relevant in dismissing the assumption that each individual holds one, overarching identity, which stays absolute across time. Instead, the study demonstrated the dynamism of processes of self-identification and the possibility that each individual can possess simultaneously several competing identities.

Recent studies also further highlight the weaknesses of conceptualising identity in Ukraine solely in terms of ethnicity or language. A study of election

---

48   Connor, W., *Ethnonationalism: The Quest for Understanding*, Princeton, NJ: Princeton University Press, 1994: 43-44.
49   Shulman, S., "The Internal-External Nexus in the Formation of Ukrainian National Identity: The Case for Slavic Integration", in Kuzio, T and D'Anieri, P., (eds.), *Dilemmas of State-Led*, 2002: 103-130.
50   Pirie, P.S., "National Identity and Politics", 1079-1104.

results published in 2000 concluded that the division between those in favour and those against Ukrainian statehood does not coincide with ethnic, nor linguistic divisions.[51] Instead, the divide may be explained with reference to regions. Moreover, Barrington analysed the results of public opinion surveys conducted in 1998 in Ukraine, which sought to examine people's support for Ukrainian independence.[52] He found that rather than ethnicity and language use being the key determinants of people's attitudes towards Ukraine as an independent state, the region of residence emerged as the chief factor. As Barrington states:

> The results indicate that, unlike other former Soviet states but like many countries in the West, the real impediments to unity in Ukraine may be related to where in the country one lives and how one is doing economically rather than who one is ethni-cally or what language one speaks.[53]

Moreover, in his study of Donbas in eastern Ukraine, Meyer argues that in this region socio-economic cleavages have been far more important than ethnic criteria for understanding processes of self-identification.[54] As Meyer states:

> Russified Ukrainians, who share many of the concerns and demands of the ethnic Russian minority, dominate the Donbass institutions. They have used their re-sources and institutional/infrastructural power to co-opt the Russian minority in an alliance, which makes political and economic demands in Kiev. However, their de-mands are not particularistic or parochially ethnic in nature. Rather, the Donbass's Russians demands are regional, economic, cultural and political (but not ethno-political). Therefore the Russians of the Donbass, find it not necessary to mobilize as Russians *per se*, but as part of a larger, multiethnic, political alliance. Indeed, it

---

51   Birch, S., *Elections and Democratisation in Ukraine*, London: MacMillan, 2000.
52   Barrington, L.W., "Region, Language, and Nationality: Rethinking Support in Ukraine for Maintaining Distance from Russia", in Kuzio, T. and D'Anieri, P., (eds.), *Dilemmas of State-Led* 131-146.
53   Barrington, L.W., "Region, Language, and Nationality: Rethinking Support in Ukraine for Maintaining Distance from Russia", in Kuzio, T. and D'Anieri, P., (eds.), *Dilemmas of State-Led,* 133.
54   According to the 1989 Soviet census, Russians comprised 44.8 percent and 43.6 percent of the populations of Luhans'k and Donets'k oblasts respectively.

seems that the Russian minority has found it more effective to pursue their ends by mobilizing around *social* ends, rather than ethnicity.[55]

The conclusions of such studies reinforce the view of Sasse that ethnic and regional fissures often crosscut rather than coincide with each other.[56] In such a way, often deep-rooted regional or sub-regional cleavages such as multi-ethnicity, cultural, historical or socio-economic factors that crosscut ethnic boundaries are disguised. Such results call into question previous attention on ethnic and linguistic divides.

1.4   Conclusions

This chapter has endeavoured to 'map' identities in Ukraine. Whilst much focus has been on ethnic and linguistic differences across Ukraine and the need to overcome these fissures in order to create a coherent Ukrainian national identity, which will promote the country's future development, such assumptions have been misplaced. This chapter argues for an examination of the 'regional' differences across Ukraine, and their effects on the state's nation-building policies.

---

55   Meyer, D.J., "Why have Donbass Russians not ethnically mobilised like Crimean Russians have? An Institutional/Demographic Approach," in his Micgiel, D.J., *State and Nation Building in East Central Europe: Contemporary Perspectives*, NY: 1996, 320.

56   Sasse, G., "The 'New' Ukraine: A State of Regions", *Regional and Federal Studies*, 11, Special Issue no. 3, Autumn 2001: 69-100.

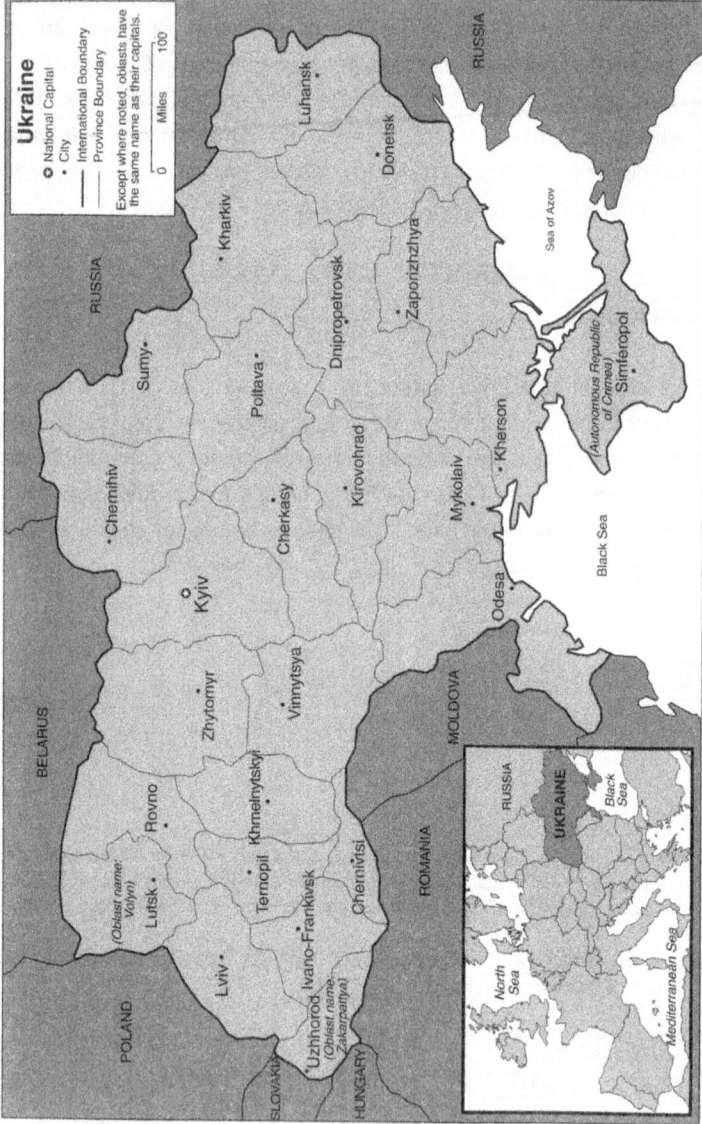

Map 1: **The territorial-administrative structure of post-Soviet Ukraine**

Source: Solchanyk, R., Ukraine & Russia: The Post-Soviet Transition. Rowman and Littlefield, Oxford, 2001.

Plate 1: **Main supermarket in the centre of Luhans'k - *Rossiya* (Russia)**

(Photographed by P.W. Rodgers, February 2003)

2   How Many Ukraines? Regionalism and the Politics of Identity

No one can really say what is happening in Ukraine, or where the country as a whole is heading – as you can in Poland, for example – because no one can grasp the country as a whole. The different areas are totally different. The people in some of them hardly know each other, and the politicians have completely different priorities. That doesn't mean that the country will break up – what happens is that the centre and the regions circle slowly around each other, trying to extract concessions. What it does mean, though, is that it makes it even more difficult to carry out economic reform – coherent economic reform, let alone radical reforms. There are just too many different interests involved all of them powerful, and none of them capable of gaining overall dominance.[57]

This chapter examines the role that the 'region' plays in Ukraine. Although much attention has focused on the 'west-east' divide, generating a series of broad generalisations, such a depiction fails to illuminate the inherent regional nuances across the country and thus highlight the actual idiosyncrasies of regional diversity across Ukraine. Instead, it is argued that as a result of Ukraine's pronounced historical diversity, there is a need to deconstruct the state into more specific, smaller regional units. However the task of defining regions in Ukraine has been far from straightforward, in a country where regional boundaries are more fluid than rigid. Various frameworks have been forwarded, dividing Ukraine according to a variety of different criteria, such as socio-economic characteristics, political persuasion, ethno-linguistic characteristics and experiences of historical rule. One of these frameworks, an eight-region model is used here as a 'skeleton' for defining regions in Ukraine.[58] To this model, the existence of a further two

---

57   Lieven, A., *Ukraine and Russia: A fraternal rivalry*, Washington DC: United States Institute of Peace Press, 1999: 79, author's interview with a Western diplomat in 1994.
58   Barrington, L.W., Herron, E.S., "One Ukraine or many? Regionalism in Ukraine and its Political Consequences", *Nationalities Papers*, 32, 1, March 2004: 53-86.

separate regions are justified, creating a model of ten regions. This chapter in particular attempts to deconstruct the notion of 'Eastern Ukraine' as a single, homogenous space. Three oblasts, all situated adjacent to the Ukrainian-Russian border, are chosen as ideal 'sites' for the focus of the study, in which local, in-depth qualitative research can take place.

2.1   Difficulties in defining Ukrainian regionalism: beyond the 'east-west' divide?

The most common manifestation of regionalism in Ukraine used by commentators has been the 'east-west' divide, in which Ukraine is portrayed as a state divided between a 'Ukrainian-speaking and nationalist west' and a 'Russian speaking and separatist east.' It is argued that such divisions have resulted from 'western Ukraine's' long interaction with Polish and Austro-Hungarian rule, and 'eastern Ukraine's' long association with Russian and Soviet rule.[59] Such a depiction of Ukraine's regional diversity became more frequent following the 1994 presidential elections, in which it was argued voting patterns could be explained by a neat divide along the River *Dnipro*, between Ukrainian speakers to the west and Russian speakers to the East.[60] Leonid Kuchma who campaigned on a platform of increasing ties with Russia won a majority in every oblast east of the river, whilst the incumbent Leonid Kravchuk who supported Ukraine's distancing from Russia won in all oblasts to the west. Overall, Kuchma won the election, thanks largely to the pure demographics of Ukraine, with more people living in the eastern than in the western regions of the country.

The 'west-east' divide was to a certain degree substantiated by research which tended to concentrate on the two cities of L'viv in the west and Donets'k in the east, seen as symbols of the two opposite poles of political

---

59   For an explanation of regional variations based on ethno-linguistic differences, see Arel, D. and Khmelko, V., "The Russian Factor and Territorial Polarisation in Ukraine", 81-91.

60   Arel, D. and Wilson, A., "The Ukrainian parliamentary elections", *RFE/RL Research Report*, 3, 26, 1994.

mobilisation in Ukraine.[61] The results of these studies highlighted how the residents of both cities hold dichotomous opinions on economic, political and geo-political preferences, thus corroborating the view that Ukraine is a country inextricably divided along an east-west axis.

Such a depiction led to commentators stating that civil war was inevitable along with the disintegration of the Ukrainian state.[62] However, what such surveys fail to do is to examine why these 'allegedly' insurmountable differences in political orientations have not manifested themselves in concerted political action. Also, by researching at the two opposite ends of the spectrum, such studies fail to examine where one 'side' ends and the 'other' starts. Indeed, Ryabchuk argues that whilst statistics demonstrate that the socio-economic, political differences between cities such as L'viv, in 'western Ukraine' and Luhans'k in 'eastern Ukraine' are striking, one cannot extrapolate these figures onto the rest of Ukrainian society so as to argue the inevitability of Ukraine's splitting into two halves.[63] Instead, it is hypothesised that these 'two Ukraines' have overlapped and fused, leaving the vast areas between them often holding characteristics of both of them, to varying degrees. In these regions, called the 'other Ukraine', 'Ukrainian' and 'Russian' and 'Soviet' and 'European' identity trajectories have interacted, leaving many Ukrainians holding very fluid and ambivalent identities.[64]

Furthermore, it has been argued that this 'myth of two Ukraines' has persisted in popular usage in Ukraine as it fits a particular viewpoint of what 'Ukraine' is and where it should be headed.[65] Zhurzhenko argues that the use of the discourse of 'Two Ukraines' has neatly fitted the bill for eastern Ukraine

---

61   Zastavnyi, F.D., *"Naselennya Ukrayiny"*, Lviv: *Prosvita*, 1993, 192, cited in Liber, G., "Imagining Ukraine: regional differences and the emergence of an integrated state identity, 1926-1994", *Nations and Nationalism*, 4:2, 1998: 187-206; also Shulman, S., "The cultural foundations of Ukrainian national identity", *Ethnic and Racial Studies*, 22, 6, November 1999: 1011-1036.

62   See Seely, R., "Ukraine's Identity Crisis", *Moscow Times*, 12 June 1994.

63   Ryabchuk, M., "Ambivalence to Ambiguity: Why Ukrainians remain undecided?", *CERI-Sciences*: 1-7.

64   Ryabchuk, M., "Ambivalence to Ambiguity", 1-7. Of course, it may well be the case that some individuals may not want to 'grab' onto any identity option, preferring to remain deeply ambivalent to political issues.

65   Zhurzhenko, T., "The myth of two Ukraines", can be found at: www.eurozine.com, accessed 17th May 2006.

to act as the 'fall guy' for difficulties encountered in nation-building processes in Ukraine post-1991. Zhurzhenko points to an article in which Ukraine has been depicted as a mixture of Estonia and Belarus, in which the inherent assumption is made that without eastern Ukraine, Ukraine would be well on its way down the 'European' path of integration. Commentating on the results of the 2002 parliamentary elections, Kuzio states,

> Nevertheless, the elections showed that west-central Ukraine voted for "Estonian-style" radical reform and a pro-Western orientation, while southern and eastern Ukraine voted along "Belarusian" lines either for a return to the communist past or for oligarchs who favour an authoritarian-corporatist state.[66]

Zhurzhenko argues that this represents an implicit effort to draw an artificial divide between 'European' Ukraine, in which civil society and democratisation are embraced against an 'Eastern' Ukraine where a primordial political culture, inherited from the Tsarist and Soviet times, prevails. As Kuzio states, "as national identities are largely absent in eastern-southern Ukraine it is little wonder that civil society is also weakest in the regions."[67] Indeed, Kuzio sees the identities of eastern Ukrainians as essentially pre-modern with their ultimate transference into a Ukrainian national one necessary as "national identities…are indispensable for political reform because only in nation-states have democracies been traditionally created."[68] However, such a deterministic approach exaggerates the importance of national identity as the only means to join the democratic European way of life. Furthermore, such simplistic over-generalisations confirm Kuzio's view of regional identities as an "indicator of an incomplete identity in transition."[69] Such an approach, whilst turning regional differences into a transitionary phenomenon, sees nation-building as a homogenising and assimilatory process, underestimating the potential for the co-existence of multiple identities in modern societies. In contrast, one must shy away from assuming that the process of nation-

66   Kuzio, T., "Election reveals Ukraine's geographic political divisions", *RFE/RL Newsline*, 6, 73, Part II, 18 April 2002.
67   Kuzio, T., *Ukraine: State and Nation Building*, London: Routledge, 1998: 162.
68   Kuzio, T., *Ukraine: State and Nation Building*, 144.
69   Kuzio, T., "National Identity in Independent Ukraine: An Identity in Transition", *Nationalism and Ethnic Politics*, 2, 4, 1996: 582-608.

building is a one-dimensional process with a preordained end. Instead, there is a need to respond to calls to take into account the complex, dynamic and multidimensional character of national identity, which cannot be reduced to a single element.[70]

2.2   The need to go deeper: the search for a regional framework?

There seems a necessity for regionalism to be seen within the prism of a graduation between the two opposing poles, with more attention placed towards an in-depth analysis of regionalism in Ukraine. Barrington analysed survey results, collected from Ukraine in late 1998, testing the effects of language use, ethnicity and region of residence on respondents' support of Ukrainian independence.[71] The results are conclusive in demonstrating the critical importance of 'region' over ethnicity or language in shaping attitudes within Ukraine as an independent country. Relating to the question of state independence, whilst the western regions were found to be more supportive than other regions, the results did not yield to a dichotomous, 'east-west' divide of the country, along the River *Dnipro*. Of particular interest, the results of Barrington's study suggested that the notion that Russophone Ukrainians think more like ethnic Russians than Ukrainophone Ukrainians was in need of re-examination.

Such a finding is significant in undermining the importance of language within the politics of identity in Ukraine. Previous studies have been quick to simplistically reduce national identity in Ukraine, to a single marker, that of language and in doing so, place both ethnic Russians and Russophone Ukrainians into a single, political grouping. For example, Arel and Wilson in their analysis of the 1994 presidential elections chose to explain the outcome of the elections by language use with Ukrainophones supporting Kravchuk

---

70   Smith, A.D., *National Identity*, London: Penguin, 1991: 14.
71   Barrington, L., "Region, Language, and Nationality: Rethinking Support in Ukraine for Maintaining Distance from Russia", in Kuzio, T. and D'Anieri, (eds.), *Dilemmas of State-Led*,131-146.

and Russophones supporting Kuchma.[72] Also, Janmaat in his study of language politics across four different cities of Ukraine, chose to analyse only the reaction of the Russophone population, making the assumption that on the basis of language usage, Ukrainians and Russians alike, hold similar political outlooks and thus would react in the same ways to state 'nationalising policies'.[73] The importance of Barrington's study is that it shed light on the blurred nature of ethnic, linguistic and regional divisions across Ukraine and in doing so highlighted the need for further detailed analysis in this area. As regards the main finding of the study, the fact that ethnic Russians in Poltava and Luhans'k may not *per se* hold similar political orientations, with instead their strongest identities being formed around their region of residence, formed through historical experience, is of great relevance.

One of the main difficulties encountered when discussing regionalism in Ukraine has been defining what actually constitutes a 'region.' Any discussion of regions in Ukraine must commence with an evaluation of the administrative structure of the country. Post-Soviet Ukraine comprises the same territorial administrative units, introduced during the Soviet period, oblasts (regions). This creates a territorial-administrative system in Ukraine comprising twenty-five oblasts and the two cities of Kiev and Sevastopol (see Map 1). However, such a system does not match the 'historical' regions of Ukraine, which often cut across the boundaries of two or more oblasts, such as Galicia, Donbas, Bukovyna and Transcarpathia.[74] However, this lack of congruence has not prevented the terms 'region' and oblast being used interchangeably in Ukrainian society. Researchers have attempted to improve understanding of the 'regional' factor in detail by defining and delineating regions on the basis of a variety of different measurements. For example, Roper and Fesnic in a study of voting behaviour chose to divide Ukraine into only two regions, on the basis of historical legacies, concentrating their analysis on differences between Galicia and the rest of Ukraine. Also Birch uses historical experience, coupled with economic development to argue for Ukraine to be split up into five regions, including, 'the former Habsburg regions in the far west',

---

72   Arel, D. and Wilson, A., "Ukraine: Back to Eurasia?", *RFE/RL Research Report*, 3, 32, 1994.
73   Janmaat, J.G., *Nation-Building in Post-Soviet Ukraine*.
74   Wolczuk, K., *Catching up with 'Europe'?*

'Western Volhynia', 'The Right Bank', 'The Left Bank' and 'The former Ottoman lands of the Black Sea littoral'.[75] Finally, Nemyria splits Ukraine into eleven regions, according to geopolitical preferences.[76] Such a variety of different schemata to define regions in Ukraine *per se* demonstrates how drawing regional boundaries in Ukraine is fraught with difficulties in a country where such boundaries are often more fluid than rigid.

Barrington and Herron have presented a new adapted framework dividing Ukraine into eight distinct regions.[77] They argue that divisions of Ukraine into macro regions such as 'Eastern Ukraine' and 'Western Ukraine' fail to illuminate inherent differentiation among areas with contrasting historical, economic and demographic profiles. The strength of their framework is the recognition of the legacies of Ukraine's historical regional diversity. It takes account of the contrasting historical experience across the territories, which comprise post-1991 independent Ukraine, which have belonged to different political entities including the Polish-Lithuanian Commonwealth, the Habsburg Empire, the Russian Empire and the Soviet Union. As Wilson sums up:

> The various regions that make up modern Ukraine have moved in and out of Ukrainian history at different times, but have never really interacted together as an ensemble... There are therefore serious difficulties in imagining Ukrainian history either as a temporal or a geographical continuum.[78]

As highlighted in Chapter 1, upon gaining independence, the post-1991 Ukrainian state found itself presiding over a citizenry whose sense of national identity was often highly fractured along ethnic, linguistic and regional lines. This framework here is used as a 'skeleton' for defining regions in Ukraine. It is critically engaged with and, when deemed appropriate, is adapted and/or adjusted with the reasoning fully explained.

---

75   Roper, S.D, and Fesnic, F., "Historical Legacies and their Impact on Post-Communist Voting Behaviour", *Europe-Asia Studies*, 55, 119-131; Birch, S., "Interpreting the Regional Effect in Ukrainian Politics", *Europe-Asia Studies*, 52, 6, 1017-1041.

76   Nemyria, G., "Regionalism: An Underestimated Dimension of State-Building", in Wolchik, S.L. and Zviglyanich, V., (eds.), *Ukraine: The Search for a National Identity*, Lanham, MA: Rowman and Littlefield, 2000: 183-198.

77   Barrington, L.W. and Herron, E.S., "One Ukraine or many?", 53-86.

78   Wilson, A., *Ukrainian Nationalism in the 1990s*, 25.

Crimea is designated as a specific region in its own right. Joining the UkrSSR in 1954, it represents the last piece in the formation of the territorial jigsaw of Ukraine in the twentieth century. According to the 1989 Soviet census, this was the only area of Ukraine, with an ethnic Russian majority, and was the only part of Ukraine, which did not wholeheartedly support independence in 1991. Since that time, the region has witnessed the formation of secessionist movements, seeking to split their allegiance away from Kiev to Moscow.[79] Indeed, the very legal status of the region, together with questions over the ownership of the Black Sea Fleet continued to sour Russian-Ukrainian relations throughout the early 1990s. According to the 2001 census, ethnic Russians remain in the majority, comprising 58.5 percent of the population with Ukrainians only 24.4 percent.[80] Amongst the local Ukrainian population, only 40.4 percent deem Ukrainian to be their native language. Moreover as the figures for the uptake of linguistic ukrainisation in schools demonstrate (see Tables 2.5 and 2.6) there has been an almost rejection of this state policy. Also of note, Crimean Tatars form 12.1 percent of the population, with their continuing resettlement on the peninsula a further issue for Kiev to deal with. Today, whilst local separatist claims have seemingly been quelled, nevertheless the area remains the most problematic, and least supportive of Ukraine's state independence.[81]

The **southern** region in the eight-region framework comprises Kherson, Odesa and Mykolaiv oblasts. These lands were absorbed into the Russian Empire in the late eighteenth century, following the conquest of the Ottoman-ruled Crimean Khanate. The region's status as 'New Russia' emerged with its rapid settlement and industrialisation, which led to large numbers of Russian migrants together with other nationalities such as Greeks, Bulgarians, Jews and Moldovans. Also, many Ukrainians migrated to the newly conquered lands, mainly to settle in the countryside. In the urban areas, Russian culture and language came to dominate. As a result of the different patterns of migration and industrialisation, the region today is less urban, and ethnically

---

79   Solchanyk, R., "The Crimean Imbroglio I: Kiev and Moscow" and "The Crimean Imbroglio II: Kiev and Simferopol", in his *Ukraine and Russia: The Post-Soviet Transition*, Lanham, MA: Rowman and Littlefield, 2001.

80   See, www.ukrcensus.gov.ua, accessed 29 April 2004.

81   Barrington, L., "Region, Language, and Nationality", 131-146.

Russian than other parts of Ukraine to the east. Whilst the issue of regional autonomy briefly surfaced in 1990/1, it has failed to grow in force in the ensuing years, other than regional elites sporadically calling for greater control over regional economic affairs. Regarding the uptake of linguistic ukrainisation in schools, of the three oblasts, only Odesa remains below the all-Ukrainian average.

The **north-central** region comprises Poltava, Kirovohrad, Cherkasy, Kiev, Chernihiv and Sumy oblasts, together with Kiev City. Until the mid-seventeenth century, these lands were mainly part of the Lithuanian-Polish Commonwealth (*Rzeczpospolita*), which was formally created at the Union of Lublin in 1569. However, Poland had great difficulties in controlling these lands, which were inhabited by Cossacks loyal to the Orthodox faith. In 1648 a revolt began aimed at defending Orthodoxy from Catholicism and against the Polish landlord-tenant system of serfdom. This revolt, however, led by Bohdan Khmelnytsk'yi, was unable to defeat Poland without any assistance. At the Union of Pereiaslav in 1654, the Cossacks entered into a union with Muscovy, one in which the Cossacks recognised the authority of the Muscovite state in return for protection and an autonomous status.[82] However, the ensuing Russian-Polish War ended with the Treaty of Andrusovo (1667), meaning this region was left under Russian control. It was allowed nominal certain rights from the onset, yet by the late eighteenth century, most of these had been taken away, in the process of fully integrating into the Russian Empire. Although these areas were under Moscow's control for a similar period of time as lands to the east and in the south, they have always retained a more 'Ukrainian' political outlook. Whilst the lands in southern and eastern Ukraine, were heavily industrialised from the late eighteenth century, the region lacked mineral resources. In contrast, their one resource of note was the land, which was of high quality and meant that agriculture played a leading role in their local economies. As such, the region was inhabited by predominantly Ukrainian peasants and saw little in-migration. During the late

---

82   Various conflicting interpretations of this event and its importance in Russian-Ukrainian relations can be found in Russian, Soviet and Ukrainian historiography. For a thorough overview of the various standpoints and the continued relevance of this period in contemporary Russian-Ukrainian relations, see Plokhy, S., "The

Tsarist and Soviet periods, the main cities in these areas came to be russified, however, barring Kiev, the cities are small in size. Overall, the population is predominantly ethnically Ukrainian, rural, and predominantly Ukrainian-speaking.

The **west-central** region comprises Zhytomyr, Vynnytsia, Khmelnytskyi, Rivne and Volyn. This region differs from the north-central region, in regard to the length of time spent under Russian and Polish rule. These areas up to the end of the eighteenth century, whilst belonging to the Polish-Lithuanian Commonwealth, underwent certain polonising processes. However, in the years 1793-1795, with the second and third partitions of Poland, they fell under Russian rule. Thus, they have been under the influence of Russian rule for much less time than those areas to the east of the river *Dnipro*. Regarding population structure, this region is predominantly rural in character. Ukrainians make up the vast majority of the population and are, in the main, Ukrainian speakers. Attempts at linguistic ukrainisation since 1991 have been embraced, with this region having scarcely any schools at all using Russian as the language of instruction. (see Tables 2.5 and 2.6). Regarding political outlook, this region is strongly supportive of Ukrainian independence. In elections since 1991, the electorate has demonstrated a rather mixed political outlook, similar to the north-central region, apart from its support for nationalist forces, although this has not been unconditional, like in the areas to its west.

Of particular relevance here, whilst Barrington and Heron include Volhyn in the **west-central** region, there are important historical distinctions from the remaining lands, providing ample justification for it to stand alone in its own right. Notably, following World War One and the creation of the USSR, the western part of **Volhyn**, fell under Polish rule. In 1944, it was then incorporated into the UkrSSR; together with the former Habsburg ruled territories. Thus, in this inter-war period, whilst areas such as Zhytomyr were being subjected to the brutal policies of Soviet modernisation, here, the traditional links with Galicia to the west were revived. These had been forcibly cut following the second partition of Poland in 1793, yet soon led to the national cause gaining a firm social base of support.

The **western** region comprises the three oblasts of L'viv, Ternopil and Ivano-Frankivs'k, which are often referred to as Galicia. As Barrington and Herron rightly note, these are the areas researchers normally consider as 'western Ukraine'. Following the downfall of the Galicia-Volhynian Princedom in 1340, these lands fell into Polish hands and by 1772, had been incorporated into the Habsburg Empire.[83] Under Habsburg rule, the national movement grew in strength as a result of the religious freedoms allowed by the authorities as well as an education system in Ukrainian and the right to use Ukrainian in public institutions. Ukrainians were allowed to develop a distinctive Ukrainian identity while maintaining a loyalty to the Habsburgs, which did not necessitate assimilation.[84] As Subtelny states, "nationally conscious Ukrainian intellectuals took advantage of the relative freedom allowed by the Habsburgs to engage in the cultural politics of nation making."[85]

Following World War One and the failed attempts to create not only an independent Ukrainian state, but also an independent West Ukrainian People's Republic (ZUNR), the region fell back under Polish rule. The Poles tried to extinguish the Ukrainian nationalist fervour, reneging on its promises in 1923 to grant Galicia a degree of autonomy and the permission to use Ukrainian language in public affairs and in the education system. However, such a policy backfired with the Galician Ukrainians reacting by remaining fiercely loyal to the Uniate Church, and radical nationalism only grew in force.

The onset of the Second World War again saw the region changing its territorial status. As a result of the Ribbentrop-Molotov Pact in 1939 between Nazi Germany and the Soviet Union, the region was incorporated into the UkrSSR. During the War years, in this region attempts were made to create an independent Ukrainian state and oppose Soviet rule. The Organisation of Ukrainian Nationalists (OUN) and Ukrainian Insurgent Army (UPA), led by Stepan Bandera, amalgamated and led a bloody campaign against both Nazi

---

83   Wilson, A., *Ukrainian Nationalism in the 1990s*, 8-9.
84   It should be noted that in the Habsburg Empire upto 1890, Ukrainians were known as 'Rusyns', or 'Ruthenians'.
85   Subtelny, O., *Ukraine: A History*, 2nd edition, Toronto: University of Toronto Press, 1992: 241-242.

German and Soviet forces during the early 1940s. The actions of these groups still remain a highly controversial part of Ukraine's history today, which is examined in greater detail in later chapters. In the post-War years Stalin tried to suppress the nationalist movement in this region by using harsh repression tactics, deportations and the forced dissolving of the Uniate Church into the Russian Orthodox Church in 1946. Yet, nationalist ideas, originating from Galicia slowly began to circulate across other areas of Ukraine, and whilst large regional differences remained, this region began to play an active role in the contestation of national identity in the UkrSSR. As Szporluk notes, the Soviet annexation of western Ukraine "may have been one of Stalin's most fateful decisions during the years from 1939 to 1945."[86]

Since 1991, this region has gained the reputation of supporting Ukrainian nationalists, whatever their levels of radicalism. Indeed, there have been worrying trends of support for the 'integral' nationalism associated with the 1930s and Dmytro Dontsov. Consequently, radical Ukrainian nationalism is often seen by Ukrainians elsewhere as a Galician product, highly influenced by its Uniate traditions and relations with Poland. In general, the region has continued to see itself as the 'Piedmont' of Ukraine, as the true keeper of national identity on behalf of the rest of Ukraine and a firm supporter of an 'away from Moscow' stance.[87] However, recently there have been growing signs of frustration with the lack of wider support for ukrainisation policies across the rest of Ukraine and the lack of movement towards Europe at a time when the region's neighbours such as Poland have been queuing up to join the European Union. The region, whilst exerting a great deal of influence on Ukrainian politics, nevertheless on the basis of its small demographic weight, is condemned to being a secondary player, trying to influence from the periphery rather than from the centre. Finally, one must be careful not to equate the superficial notion 'western Ukraine' solely with this region. The high levels of nationalist support here are linked to this region's specific historical characteristics and for varying reasons do not gain the same levels of appeal across other neighbouring regions.

---

86   Szporluk, R., "The Soviet West-or Far Eastern Europe?", in *East European Politics and Societies*, 5, 3, 1991: 466-482.
87   This refers to the model of Italian unification by the House of Savoy in 1860.

In Barrington and Herron's eight-region framework, a **south-west** region is denoted, comprising the Chernivtsi and Zakarpatia oblasts, where owing to historical reasons, the levels of "Ukrainianness" are lower than in Galicia.[88] Both oblasts share similarities in having long external borders and subsequently, large numbers of national minorities, including Hungarians, Slovaks, and Romanians. Nevertheless, this author feels that also there are strong reasons, as a result of divergent historical experiences, to legitimate splitting it into two, distinct regions, as explained below.

Bukovyna has long been a disputed territory. Up to 1918 along with Galicia, was part of the Habsburg Empire. However, whilst in the late nineteenth century in Galicia, the Ukrainian national idea rapidly gained strength, here with the emergence of an independent Romanian state in 1858, a viable alternative national project was available for the region's inhabitants. Also, in contrast to Galicia, the Orthodox Church remained in the ascendancy.[89] Following World War One, these lands were incorporated into the Romanian state, which quickly began to pursue stringent 'romanianisation' policies in the cultural and linguistic spheres. However, as a result of the Molotov-Ribbentrop Pact, in 1940, it joined the UkrSSR, an administrative change which was made permanent in 1945. Since 1991, the region has witnessed the co-existence of a reviving Ukrainian nationalism and also a strong minority, Romanian nationalism. In particular, some autonomous trends have been exhibited, with local Romanian nationalists calling for the establishment of a Romanian university in Chernivtsi and even joint Romanian-Ukrainian citizenship. In areas where a Romanian and Moldovan population predominates, local self-government has been granted.[90]

Zakarpatiya was also previously part of the Habsburg Empire, and was part of Hungary, Czechoslovakia, Romania and Nazi Germany, before joining the UkrSSR in 1945.[91] Indeed, in 1938/9, the region even flirted with outright independence forming the Republic of Carpatho-Ukraine. The chief distinguishing feature of this region is its ethnic diversity, with over one hundred

---

88   Barrington, L.W, and Herron, E.S., "Region, Language, and Nationality", 59.
89   Wilson, A., *The Ukrainians: unexpected nation*, 115.
90   Bugajski, J., "Ethnic Relations and Regional Problems in Independent Ukraine", in Wolchik, S.L. and Zviglyanich, V., *Ukraine: The Search for a National Identity*, Lanham, MA: Rowman and Littlefield, 2000:178.

representatives of different nationalities residing in the oblast.[92] According to the 2001 census, Ukrainians comprise 80.5 percent of the population, with Hungarians making up 12.1 percent, representing the largest minority group.[93] However, the Ukrainian population is itself split between Ukrainians and Rusyns, who argue that they are a separate ethnic identity and thus demand political recognition of this fact. Also, internal splits within the Rusyn community along cultural, political and generational lines have hampered their political development since 1991.[94] Autonomist tendencies have also arisen here, with various groups calling for varying degrees of self-determination. Indeed, in a special referendum in December 1991, over 78 percent of the population voted for the creation of a "special self-governing administrative territory", yet within the overall framework of an independent Ukraine. The Hungarian minority has also been extremely active, calling for greater autonomy in the Berehiv (Berehovo) *raion* (district), where Hungarians are compactly settled.[95] Such demands are also supported by the Hungarian government, which has built friendly bilateral relations with Ukraine, on the proviso that this minority is given certain rights and protection. The mixed nature of the population to an extent is mirrored in the voting patterns of the electorate. In contrast to the neighbouring western region, where nationalists have been strongly supported, here the nationalist support is more lukewarm, with the centrist parties instead gaining much support.

The **eastern** region comprises Donets'k and Luhans'k oblasts, which represent the Ukrainian part of the Donbas coal basin, which spans the Russian and Ukrainian border. Nemyria, focusing on the Donbas region, argues that territorial and economic factors have been more important than ethnic and linguistic factors in explaining factors of self-identification.[96] He

---

91   Sasse, G., "The 'New' Ukraine: A State of Regions", 82.
92   See, www.ukrcensus.gov.ua, accessed 18 May 2004.
93   *Ibid.*
94   Batt, J., "Transcarpathia: Peripheral Region at the 'Centre of Europe' ", in Batt, J. and Wolczuk. K., (eds.), *Regions, State and Identity in Central and Eastern Europe*, London and Portland, OR: Frank Cass, 2002.
95   Berehiv is the name of the district in Ukrainian, whilst Berehovo is the Hungarian name.
96   Nemyria, G., "A Qualitative Analysis of the Situation in the Donbas", in Segbers, K. and De Spiegelaire, S., (eds.), *Emerging Geopolitical and Territorial Units. Theories, Methods and Case Studies. Post-Soviet Puzzles. Mapping the Political Econ-*

states how there exists a specific regional identity in Donbas, which has been heavily conditioned by the history of its development in the USSR. Donbas in the USSR was the showcase of socialism, a privileged place that led to its inhabitants proudly stating that they were from the *Vsyesoyuznaya Kochegarka* (boiler room of the whole union).[97] Nemyria defines the peculiarity of this Donbas identity when he states:

> For the Donbas, the real economic and political centre was the Soviet one, in Moscow. Kiev was just the regional administrative centre, not of great importance. So when we became independent, there had to be a major and very difficult re-evaluation of which centre to look to. It was made even more complicated by the fact that for us here, regional identity was always more important than national identity. The fact that you came from the Donbas was more important than that you were Russian or Ukrainian; so of course the break-up of the Soviet Union also meant a raising of this regional identity and loyalty...In any case, most people here honestly couldn't say what they are ethnically, because most families, like mine, are mixed.[98]

It would be mistaken to simplistically see the region as a unilaterally 'pro-Russian, Russian speaking' region. Indeed, election results since 1991 have shown that there has been hardly any support for pro-Russian nationalist parties in both Luhans'k and Donets'k oblasts.

The **east-central** region constitutes Zaporizhzhia, Dnipropetrovs'k and Kharkiv oblasts. In contrast to the Donbas region to the east, in these areas, there is little dispute that they were once part of a historical Ukrainian or proto-Ukrainian state. In addition, although this region is industrial and russified in both cultural and linguistic terms, it is not to such a high degree as in the Donbas. Moreover, the agricultural sector plays an important role in the local economies. Consequently, whilst the region has consistently voted for left-wing forces, there has been more of a mixture of moderate and 'hard left' forces gaining support in elections. Similarly, as portrayed in Tables 2.5 and 2.6, whilst these three oblasts are still below the all-Ukrainian average,

---

omy of the Former Soviet Union, vol.2, Baden and Baden: Nomos Verlagsgellschaft, 1995: 57-58.

97   Nemyria, G., "Regionalism: An Underestimated Dimension of State-Building", 190.
98   Nemyria is quoted in Lieven, A., *Ukraine and Russia: A fraternal Rivalry*, 80.

nevertheless, since 1991, there has been a steady embrace of linguistic ukrainisation.

To sum up, Barrington and Herron provide a sound framework, which importantly takes into account the divergent historical experiences of Ukraine's regions. The strength of the framework is that it deconstructs concepts such as 'western Ukraine' and 'eastern Ukraine' with sound justifications. However, as argued above, it does have shortcomings, requiring adjustments. In particular, the author has argued that Volhyn, Zakarpatiya and Bukovyna, while holding similarities with neighbouring areas, nevertheless owing to specific historical and demographic reasons, merit the status as regions in their own right. Overall, this framework and the modifications to it, provide a useful point of reference for research into regionalism in Ukraine. However, it is also imperative to take into account Birch's argument for the need to find *explanations* for, and the *meanings* of, regional differences.[99]

2.3   From the macro to the micro: meaning and perception at the local level

Jackson argues that rather than scientifically measuring the effect of regional differences in countrywide opinion polls and surveys at the macro level, more research should focus on the *perceptions* of these differences at the micro level.[100] In doing so, important insights can be gained into how the state-led nation-building project is negotiated and shaped at the local level. Jackson within her study of Zaporizhzhia, found that the area was not quintessentially 'pro-Russian, anti-Ukrainian language and history', as is stereotyped in the 'east-west' divide. Instead, it was noted how the specific Cossack heritage of the city was being used to increase the sense of affiliation to Ukrainian culture and language. Similarly, Jackson argues that subtle differences exist within and between regions at the local level, often in politically considered 'less active' areas such as Zaporizhzhia but are often

---

99   Birch, S., "Interpreting the Regional Effect in Ukrainian Politics", 1023.
100   Jackson, L., *The Construction of National Identity in Ukraine*, 182-183.

masked by the macro-level studies.[101] As regards the significance of such findings, the consequences for the Ukrainian state in its nation building project are unclear. On the one hand, one can argue that the complex nature of regional divisions in Ukraine and a lack of a real dichotomous 'east-west' divide should bring greater stability to the country and reduce fears of a potential split of the country along the Dnipro river. However, the presence of such fuzzy and blurred regional identities, which crisscross not only oblast boundaries, but also possibly international state boundaries, makes the state's task of providing an all-embracing all-Ukrainian national identity far from straightforward.

It may be the case that there exists a type of *'transnational regionalism'* in areas close to Ukraine's state borders, defined by a high level of social interaction across the state boundaries.[102] Regional studies, for example, in Russia have highlighted the emergence of transnational regions and regional identities.[103] Indeed, a survey undertaken in 1996 demonstrated that the majority of the citizens of Ukraine and Russia do not identify with their new states as their homelands, with regional identities and Soviet identities instead proving highly popular.[104] As such, whilst the vast majority of citizens in Ukraine hold a territorial attachment to Ukraine, nevertheless the state boundary does not necessarily coincide with borders symbolically constructed by the population itself. As Laba states:

> Borders are supposed to be focal points for conflicting historical memories and political wills of nations and states. They make concrete: what is my country and who is the other. They are physical manifestations of national and state identity. The peculiarity of the Ukrainian-Russian relationship is that there is a physical state

---

101   Jackson, L., "Identity, Language and Transformation in Eastern Ukraine: Case Study of Zaporizhzhia", in Kuzio, T., (ed.), *Contemporary Ukraine*, 99-113.

102   Hurrell, A., "Explaining the resurgence of regionalism in World Politics", *Review of International Studies*, 21, October 1995: 333.

103   Bradshaw, M., and Makarychev, A., "Globalization and Fragmentation: The Impact of the International Relations of Russia's Regions", in Ruble, B., Koehn, J. and Popson, N., (eds.), *Fragmented Spaces in the Russian Federation*, Washington DC: Woodrow Wilson Center Press, 2001.

104   Holovaha, Y. and Panina, N., "Tendentsii Rozvytku Ukrayinsko-Rosiyskykh Vidnosyn u Hromadskyi Dumtsi Rosii ta Ukrayiny," 1998, http://niurr.gov.ua/ukr/zbirka/golovpan.html, quoted in Wolczuk, K., "History, Europe and the 'National Idea'", 671-694.

border, while a large minority in Ukraine and an overwhelming majority on the Russian side see no significant reason for its existence. For many people, there is no difference to express, no reason for the borders.[105]

This chapter progresses with an examination of three chosen study areas, the cities of Luhans'k, Kharkiv and Sumy, capitals of their respective oblasts, all situated along the Ukrainian-Russian borderland yet situated in different regions according to the '8-10' classification. Luhans'k is situated in the eastern region, Kharkiv in the east-central and Sumy in the north-central region.

2.4   Ukraine's eastern borderlands

To deconstruct the notion of 'Eastern Ukraine' as a single and homogenous space, this study focuses research at the local level in three oblast capitals, namely Luhans'k, Kharkiv and Sumy (see Map 1). Following Ukraine's independence in 1991, the number of oblasts, which hold external borders, rose from five to sixteen.[106] Such changes have instigated a realignment of how regions define themselves and perceive their interests *vis-à-vis* the centre in Kiev. In particular, these areas have external borders with Russia and also are regions where 'multiple' or 'hybrid' identities prevail.[107] Such identities have resulted from the erosion of linguistic and cultural boundaries between Russians and Ukrainians under Tsarist and more particularly Soviet 'russification' policies. A key component of the state-led nation-building project in Ukraine has been the state's efforts to reinvent and recodify social boundaries that distinguish 'us' from 'them', portraying Russia as the 'other'. Thus, these three oblasts provide an ideal testing ground to see to what extent Russia is perceived as the 'other' at the micro level and how state representations of Russia as the 'other' are negotiated and

---

105   Laba, R., "The Russian-Ukrainian Conflict: State, Nation and Identity", *European Security*, 4, 3, 1995: 478.

106   Birch, S., and Zinko, I., "The dilemmas of regionalism", *Transition*, November 1998: 22-25.

107   Szporluk, R., "Ukraine: from an imperial periphery to a sovereign state", *Daedalus*, 126, 3, 1997: 85-119.

contested. Moreover, this research focuses on people's *perceptions* of regional and national divisions and the meanings attached to them. In this way, one can provide a comparative perspective, evaluating the dynamics of the nation-building project. The results from this study will feed into state-wide debates surrounding the politics of identity in Ukraine and the role that the 'region' plays in such debates.

Moreover, choosing these three borderland areas contributes to a body of work, centred around the work of Sahlins, which looks at the role of borderlands within processes of national identity formation and change.[108] Furthermore, this study aims to add to the body of work regarding the importance of borderlands as constituents of collective identities, which recognise the social construction of boundaries.[109]

Since the disintegration of the Soviet Union and the imposition of an international border between Ukraine and Russia, the Russian and Ukrainian borderland regions have begun to face two contradictory processes. On the one hand, concerted attempts have begun to 'nationalise' the borderlands, a process in which the state invests symbolically so that public perceptions coincide with realities regarding the extent of state territories. Simultaneously a drive has commenced in the local areas towards (re)building economic and social ties with their neighbouring areas on the basis of cross-border co-operation and also a reinterpretation of regional histories and identities.[110] Thus, of particular relevance, whilst the Ukrainian state is attempting to produce a unified Ukrainian historical narrative, such efforts may not be insulated from competing narratives of Russian-Ukrainian historical relations, present in Russia and prevailing in these borderland regions.

---

108 Sahlins, P., *Boundaries: The Making of France and Spain in the Pyrenees*, Berkeley, CA: University of California Press, 1989.

109 Donnan, H. and Wilson, T.M., (eds.) *Border Approaches: Anthropological Perspectives on Frontiers*, Lanham, MA: University Press of America, 1994; Paasi, A., *Territories, Boundaries and Consciousness: The Changing Geographies of the Finnish-Russian Border*, New York: John Wiley, 1996.

110 Zhurzhenko, T., "Part 1: Cross-border Cooperation and Transformation of Regional Identities in the Ukrainian-Russian Borderlands: Towards a Euroregion 'Slobozhanshchina' ", *Nationalities Papers*, 32, 1, March 2004: 207-231.

2.4.1 Luhans'k

To fully understand the socio-political dynamics of Luhans'k oblast, it is necessary to recognise significant differences between its southern and northern parts. The southern parts are highly urbanised, a factor explained by the highly industrialised nature of this area, which forms part of the Donbas region straddling the Russian-Ukrainian border and of which 85 percent is situated in the Ukrainian oblasts of Donets'k and Luhans'k. In contrast, the northern part, historically part of the *Slobozhanshchyna* region, is more rural with its local economies predominantly based around agriculture. In fact, pre-1917, whilst the northern parts of today's oblast were part of the Kharkiv *guberniia* (province) from 1835, the southern parts were part of the Katerynoslav (Ekaterinislav) *guberniia*. However after 1919, the majority of the area became part of the Donets'k *guberniia*, which became the Donets'k oblast in 1932. By 1938, the administrative boundaries had changed again, with the division of Donets'k oblast into Stalino (now Donets'k) and Voroshy-lovhrad (now Luhans'k) oblasts.[111] In the post-war years, Luhans'k was the object 'russification' processes coupled with Soviet urbanisation and industri-alisation. In particular, figures regarding the proportion of children learning in Ukrainian language schools in the region demonstrate a fall from 40.5 percent in 1951/2 to only 8.5 percent in 1985/6. In city of Luhans'k itself, by 1986, there were no Ukrainian language schools remaining.[112]

Regarding the role of the area in Ukrainian politics, it is first worthwhile stressing that in the uncertain years preceding the collapse of the Soviet Union, a local movement known as the Democratic Movement of Donbass, was formed in Luhans'k in 1990. It called on the electorate to reject Ukrainian independence and instead proposed the formation of an autonomous Donets'k-Krivoi Rog region as a constituent part of a federated Ukraine within the USSR.[113] However, the results of the December 1991 referendum, were unexpected by the analysts. The population of Luhans'k oblast along with all

---

111   Kuromiya, H., *Freedom and Terror in the Donbas: A Ukrainian-Russian Borderland, 1870s-1990s*, Cambridge: Cambridge University Press, 1998, xii.

112   Arel, D., *Language and the Politics of Ethnicity: The Case of Ukraine*, University of Illinois (PhD dissertation), 1993.

113   *Vechirnii Kiev*, 4 October 1991, quoted in Solchanyk, R., "The Politics of State Building: Centre Periphery Relations in Post-Soviet Ukraine", *Europe-Asia Studies*, 46, 1, 1994: 42-68.

the other eastern areas strongly voted in favour of Ukrainian independence, a result in hindsight, which was put down to the expectation that independence, would bring greater prosperity and stability.[114]

However, during the initial years of independence, the deteriorating economic situation led to regional activism sprouting in the Luhans'k and Donets'k regions. Demands included more regional autonomy, particularly in the economic sphere, closer links with Russia and the neighbouring Russian regions and calls for the Russian language to be elevated to the status of a state language alongside Ukrainian.[115] Such demands created an element of fear in Kiev that the region would break away from Ukraine and join Russia. In particular, such fears were exacerbated during the run-up to the 1994 parliamentary elections, when both Donets'k and Luhans'k oblast councils voted overwhelmingly for the state status for the Russian language.[116] However, post-1994 such fears have increasingly come to be seen as unjustified with political mobilisation in Donbas generally calling for greater political, economic or cultural autonomy rather than outright secession. Yet simultaneously regional elites in Donbas have used such sentiments as a bargaining card during interactions with the political centre. Indeed the failure of a secessionist movement has been explained by the region's peculiar characteristics.[117]

Sasse argues that political mobilisation in the Donbas region has been linked to Soviet institutional legacies, the region's socio-economic profile and the specifics of the regional elites. In the Soviet times, the regional elites formed an integral part of the Soviet *nomenklatura* and thus looked primarily to Moscow for career elevation and central state subsidies for the large industrial enterprises under their tutelage. However, in the post-Soviet years, whilst the regional elites have had to orientate themselves more to Kiev in the

---

114   In Luhans'k region, 83.3 percent of people voted for independence. For the other regional results and a comprehensive overview of the period leading upto Ukrainian independence, see Nahaylo, B., *The Ukrainian Resurgence*, London: Hurst, 1999.

115   For an in-depth examination of the developments at this time in Donbas, see Wilson, A., "The Growing Challenge to Kiev from the Donbas", *RFE/RL Research Report*, 20 August 1993: 8-13.

116   Jung, M., "The Donbas Factor in the Ukrainian Elections", *RFE/RL Research Report*, 25 March 1994: 52-53.

117   Sasse, G., "The 'New' Ukraine: A State of Regions", 86.

bargaining process for continued subsidies, nonetheless close links to Russia have remained. In Luhans'k oblast, regional authorities have indeed been keen to maintain strong links with the neighbouring Russian regions, leading to analysts calling Luhans'k the "eastern gates of Ukraine."[118] Also, the old links with Moscow remain, highlighted by the latest visit by the Mayor of Moscow, Yurii Luzhkov, to the 2003 celebrations of the 65th anniversary of the foundation of Luhans'k oblast.

In fact, the peculiar nature of multiple identities in Luhans'k, as opposed to clear-cut ethnic or ethnolinguistic identities, has led to a near-total lack of support for Russian nationalist agendas in election since 1994. Thus, descriptions of parts of eastern Ukraine being bastions of 'pro-Russian separatists' have proved to be misplaced. Instead, the population has strongly backed left-wing forces, notably the hard left KPU, gaining the reputation as being the 'red pole of Ukraine'.[119] To understand such results, one needs to take into account the socio-economic characteristics of the region. Since 1991, the economy has declined considerably suffered, with numerous closures of old Soviet behemoth industrial complexes and coal-mines and decline in the Ukrainian agricultural sector. Such changes have left much of the population living in severe poverty, a situation that the Commu-nists have been quick to exploit, advocating a return to the Soviet economic system and a decent welfare system. For example, in the 1998 parliamentary elections, KPU polled 45.98 percent in the region, the highest figure recorded across Ukraine.

In the parliamentary elections in 2002, the results in Luhans'k were ex-tremely revealing.[120] Whilst across many regions of Ukraine, there was strong support for Viktor Yushchenko's *Nasha Ukrayina* (Our Ukraine) bloc, who advocated political and economic reforms and a strong 'European' orientation in foreign policy, in Luhans'k support was virtually non-existent. Only in Luhans'k, in neighbouring Donets'k oblast and the City of Sevastopol did *Nasha Ukrayina* not gain 4 percent of the vote. In fact, of significance has

---

118   "'Skhidni vorota Ukrayini': kudi voni vedut?", *Ukryains'kii rehional'nii visnik*, 38, 1 November 2001, *Institut Skhid-Zakhid*.

119   "Politichni obrii Luhanshchyni", *Ukrayins'kii rehional'nii visnik*, 38, November 2001, *Institut Skhid-Zakhid*.

been the total lack of support for any national-democratic forces in any of the elections. In contrast, KPU (Communist Party of Ukraine) received 39.69 percent of the vote, the highest vote in any region of Ukraine, with the remaining vote spread out across the pro-Presidential oligarchic parties ZYU (For One Ukraine) (14.38 percent) and SDPU–o (Social Democratic Party of Ukraine–united) (9.44 percent).

Furthermore, in the Presidential elections of 2004, the current President Yushchenko gained a tiny 6.22 percent whilst Yanukovych, advocating closer ties with Russia and introducing Russian as a second state language in Ukraine, gained an overwhelming 91.25 percent of the vote (Table 2.1). Such results demonstrated not only the strong hold that Yanukovych, with his support base centred in nearby Donets'k, had on Luhans'k oblast, but also that his pro-Russian message struck a strong chord here. Conversely, even though Yushchenko was actually born in Sumy oblast, certain sections of the Ukrainian media and much of the Russian media's branding of him as a 'wild, western-Ukrainian nationalist' deeply eroded the chance of any support here, demonstrating the fact that 'nationalism' in the highly sovietised Donbas, remains a 'dirty' word. Similarly in the Parliamentary elections of 2006 and 2007, Yanukovych's Party of the Regions, gained resounding votes of 74.33 and 73.53 per cent respectively in the oblast, with more 'national-democratic' parties, in the form of 'BYUT', led by Yuliya Tymoshenko and *Nasha Ukrayina* (Our Ukraine) gaining a tiny percentage of the vote (Table 2.2).

Such results point to the local population's general apprehensive stance towards the ukrainisation policies, proposed by national-democratic forces. This fact is backed up by the results of attempts to ukrainianise the education system since 1991. In Luhans'k oblast, in 1991/2, the proportion of children attending Ukrainian language schools was 6.7 percent, but after a decade of assertive state-sponsored linguistic ukrainisation policies by 2000/1, it had only risen to 17 percent, still well below the proportion of ethnic Ukrainians in the local population.[121] (see Tables 2.4 and 2.6). Even more striking were the

---

120   The results can be found on Ukraine's Central Elections Committee webpage, http://www.cvkukrpack.net, accessed 7 August 2002.
121   "Systema osvity v Ukrayini: stan ta perspectyvy posvytku", in *National'na bespeka / oborona*, 4, 28, 2002: 8, Ukrayins'kyi tsentr ekonomichnix i politichnix doslidzhen' imeni Oleksandra Razumkova.

figures concerning language of instruction in pre-school education establish-ments for 2000.[122] Whilst across Ukraine, there had been a dramatic increase in the use of Ukrainian, and also in other 'russified' regions, such as Zaporizhzhia and Donets'k, where 62.9 percent and 34.5 percent of children were being taught in Ukrainian, Luhans'k was lagging a long way behind at only 19.7 percent. (see Tables 2.3 and 2.5).

The region's strong attachment to the Russian language and stuttering embrace of ukrainisation is again seen in the results of the recent 2001 National Ukrainian Census.[123] In terms of nationality, Ukrainians comprise 58 percent of the population, an increase of 6.1 percent from the previous 1989 Soviet census, with the proportion of Russians falling from 44.8 to 39 percent. However, the results concerning native language (*ridna mova* in Ukrainian and *rodnoi yasyk* in Russian) are extremely revealing. Ukrainian is regarded as the native language for only 30 percent of the region's population, repre-senting *an actual fall* of 4.9 percent since 1989. In direct contrast, Russian is regarded as the native language for 68.8 percent of the population, a rise of 4.9 percent since 1989. Within these figures, the percentage of Ukrainians who view Ukrainian as their native language stands at only 50.6 percent with 49.4 percent seeing Russian as their native language. Thus, these results seemingly reveal two trends in the region. In the post-1991 period of Ukrain-ian independence, many people have renegotiated their identities, increas-ingly seeing themselves as Ukrainians. However, such shifts have not coincided with a shift towards the Ukrainian language. Thus, seemingly one can draw the tentative conclusion that whilst people may be coming to view themselves as 'Ukrainian', a specific regional version of Ukrainian identity exists here, which is not viewed in solely linguistic terms.

Also whilst in many other cities across Ukraine since independence there have been concerted efforts to destroy the past signs of Russian/Soviet influence involving the changing of street names and the pulling down of statues commemorated to Communist heroes, in Luhans'k, this process has not occurred. The city's main thoroughfare, *Ulitsya Sovetskaya* (Soviet Street) remains so does the hotel also of this name. Also, Soviet monuments

---

122   *Ibid.*, 5.
123   Results can be found at, www.ukrcensus.gov.ua, accessed 29 April 2004.

including those to Lenin and also Feliks Dzerzhinsky, the infamous founder of the NKVD (forerunner to the KGB) is still intact. Furthermore, the city's close links with Russia are highlighted in the name of the main supermarket in the city being simply *Rossiya* (Russia) (see Plate 2.1).

During the Soviet times, the region, in the main being part of the Don-bas, received the full force of Soviet modernisation processes, particularly in terms of linguistic and cultural 'russification.' Yet, this region should not be seen as holding an exclusive 'Russian' character, but rather a blurred mixture of Russian and Ukrainian identities, with association with the Soviet Union, still strong amongst the older generations and the economically least well off.

However, in elections the population has emphatically failed to support explicitly pro-Russian nationalist forces. Instead, the region has supported hard-line leftist forces and simultaneously rejected national-democratic forces. Such results, coupled with the historical legacies of the region's specific role and development under both Tsarist and Soviet rule explain the population's negotiation of state-led linguistic ukrainisation. Whilst the region has not wholly rejected it, it has been more backward than forward in its uptake.

2.4.2 Kharkiv

The history of this area is closely tied with the history of *Sloboz-hanshchya*. Located south east of the Hetmanate and to the south and west of the Belgorod defensive line, it was settled in the mid seventeenth century by Ukrainian peasants and Russian settlers on the borderlands of Muscovy, Poland and the Tatar Khanate.[124]

As a border region, *Slobozhanshchyna* attracted many peasants and Cossacks, fleeing from religious and social violence in Polish controlled regions of today's Ukraine. Under Tsarist rule, Kharkiv developed rapidly, being considerably larger than Kiev for much of this period. During the twentieth century, Kharkiv was the first capital of the UkrSSR from 1918-1934 and grew to become a major centre for the military-industrial complex and also a major cultural, transportation and intellectual centre. Also the national

---

124   Leckey, C., "Provincial Readers and Agrarian Reform, 1760s-1770s: The Case of Sloboda Ukraine", *Russian Review*, 61, October 2002: 535-559.

composition of the region's population in this period changed greatly. As a result of the influx of Russian migrants and 'russification' policies, between 1959 and 1989, the proportion of Ukrainians fell from 82.2 to 63.1 percent. In contrast, the proportion of Russians rose from 17.2 percent to 33.4 percent. In terms of language instruction in schools, the proportion of children in Ukrainian language schools fell from 71.8 percent in 1951/2 to 27.9 percent in 1985/6.[125]

Indeed, an ethnographic study of the Russian-Ukrainian borderlands in the late 1980s found that the population of the region had a culture, local traditions and a mentality, which is difficult to define as either Russian or Ukrainian.[126]

The historical settlement of this region has been hotly debated since the nineteenth century with key issues including to what extent is *Sloboz-hanshchyna* was from the onset, a truly 'Ukrainian' land. Was the region 'russified' by forced pressure from the Tsarist and Soviet regimes, or does the history's multiethnic character stem from the joint and natural settlement of the region by both Russians and Ukrainians? However, in the post-1991 period, such debates have become far more vocal. Indeed, Zhurzhenko notes that whilst the 'Ukrainian' character of the region has been expressed in certain circles, this has come to be contested by a powerful 'multicultural' discourse.[127] This version of historical events has been co-opted by regional elites who have used it to create a compromised version of the 'national idea' for the region. *Slobozhanshchyna* has been (re)invented as an alternative to a 'national idea' determined by solely ethnic and linguistic markers. In particular, it provides a strong counter-argument to those who claim that blurred identities in eastern Ukraine represent the pollution of Ukrainian identities by Russian/Soviet influence, and highlight the unfinished nature of the nation-building project.[128]

---

125   Arel, D., "Language Politics in Independent Ukraine: Towards One or Two State Languages?", *Nationalities Papers*, 3, 1994: 597-622.
126   Chizhykova, L.N., "Russkoe-Ukrainskoe pogranich'e", 49.
127   Zhurzhenko, T., "Cross-border Cooperation and Transformation of Regional Identities in the Ukrainian-Russian Borderlands: Towards a Euroregion "Sloboz-hanshchya?", Parts 1 and 2, *Nationalities Papers*, 32, 1, March 2004: 207-231.
128   Kuzio, T., *Ukraine: State and Nation Building,* London: Routledge, 1998: 162.

In contrast, the 'multicultural' discourse rejects the claims that imperial and colonial masters forcibly imposed Russian influence in the region. In this way, a specific regional identity is being espoused which while endorsing the original 'Ukrainian' character of the region, highlights the traditional Russian-Ukrainian friendly relations in the region. This therefore justifies Kharkiv's role as the mediator of relations between Russia and Ukraine and the significant regional efforts undertaken to create further cross-border co-operation. In particular, the pro-presidential ZYU (For One Ukraine) party's slogan in the region at the recent 2002 parliamentary elections was "Kharkiv is the capital of Ukrainian-Russian co-operation." Such slogans were adorned around the centre of the city when the author visited it in 2002 (see Plate 2.2). Of interest, the slogan was written on one side in the Ukrainian language and on the other, in Russian, highlighting also the specific linguistic situation of the city.

Regarding voting patterns since 1991, Kharkiv has generally supported left-wing forces, yet subtle differences can be seen in comparison to the results from Luhans'k. In the 1998 parliamentary elections, whilst the KPU gained 35.4 percent of the vote, other more moderate left-wing forces and centrist forces also gained substantial support.[129] Similarly in the 2002 parliamentary elections, whilst the KPU vote still led with 30.69 percent, the pro-presidential parties of ZYU and SDPU-o (Social Democratic Party of Ukraine–united) gained 15.38 and 10.35 percent respectively.[130] In contrast to its appalling showing in Luhans'k, *Nasha Ukrayina* gained 5.92 percent of the vote, which can probably be put down to votes from the city's large intelligentsia.

Furthermore, regarding the 2004 Presidential elections in Kharkiv oblast, whilst the majority of voters supported Yanukovych's desire to maintain close ties with Russia, over a quarter of voters here were willing to engage with and support Yushchenko's vision for a European-orientated, democratic Ukraine, ideas which were outwardly rejected in Luhans'k (Table 2.1). Moreover, in the Parliamentary elections in 2006 and 2007 respectively, whilst support for the Party of the Regions was strong at 51.7 and 49.61

---

129   Craumer, P.R. and Clem, J.I., "Ukraine's emerging Electoral Geography": 16.
130   Results at Ukraine's Central Elections Commissions website, http://www.cvk. ukrpack.net, 7 August 2002.

percent, the 'national democratic' forces here were not totally overwhelmed as in Luhans'k, with Tymoshenko's BYUT gaining a respectable 12.68 percent in 2006 and 16.36 percent of the vote in 2007 (Table 2.2).

Concerning changes in the composition of the population, in 2001, Ukrainians comprised 70.7 percent a rise of 7.9 percent from the previous 1989 census, with Russians in contrast comprising 25.6 percent, down from 33.2 percent in 1989.[131] Regarding language, across the oblast, 53.8 percent saw Ukrainian as their native language, a rise of 3.3 percent from 1989. Amongst Ukrainians, 74.1 percent saw Ukrainian as their native language and 25.8 percent Russian. Also, in terms of language instruction in schools, whilst in 1985/6, only 27.9 percent of children went to Ukrainian language schools, by 2000/1, this figure had risen to 55 percent. (see Tables 2.4 and 2.6). Also, in the pre-school establishments, by 2000, 82.7 percent of children were instructed in Ukrainian, a figure in fact higher than the proportion of Ukrainians in the local population.[132] (see Tables 2.3 and 2.5). These figures show, in comparison to those from Luhans'k, a much more enthusiastic uptake of linguistic Ukrainian.

Such trends are supported by the results of some qualitative research, undertaken in Kharkiv in 2003.[133] Sovik found after carrying out in-depth interviews with teenagers that although the Ukrainian language was not being fully embraced, nevertheless certain trends were becoming apparent. In particular, Sovik argues that certainly for some interviewees the Ukrainian language had taken on the role as a symbol of Ukrainian identity, even though these individuals continued to use the Russian language in everyday life. Other individuals stated how whilst their use of the Russian language formed a part of their 'personal' identity, something that linked them to a wider East-Slavic community, nevertheless, the Ukrainian language was still seen as significant, as representing the Ukrainian state. In this manner, one can see a slight difference in attitudes in Kharkiv compared to Luhans'k. In Luhans'k, there was strong resistance to state attempts at linguistic ukrainisa-

---

131   www.ukrcensus.gov.ua, accessed 29 April 2004.

132   "Systema osvity v Ukrayini: stan ta perspectyvy rosvytku", 5.

133   Sovik, M., "Who am I? Perceptions of language and identity among students in Kharkiv", paper presented at a conference, organised by the Centre for Border

tion, in Kharkiv, although the majority of the population still continues to use the Russian language in their everyday lives, they are more open and willing to embrace the state's linguistic ukrainisation project.

2.4.3 Sumy

From the ninth century, part of Sumy oblast was part of the Pereiaslav and Chernihiv principalities in the kingdom of Kiev Rus' and in the mid twelfth century, part of the Novgorod-Siversky principality. During these times, many settlements were created, but a century later many had suffered severely at the hands of the Tatar invaders. By the mid fourteenth century, much of present day Sumy oblast had been captured by the Lithuanian principality, which stayed under their tutelage until the peace treaty of 1503 when much of the land was absorbed into the Muscovite state.[134] The sixteenth and seventeenth centuries witnessed the growth of many settlements in this area, often fortresses acting as important border points between the Polish and Russian controlled parts of modern day Ukraine. Under Tsarist control, the area was absorbed into the Kharkiv *guberniia* and the city slowly developed with its industrial enterprises engaged in agricultural production and processing, providing for the needs of the surrounding rural, agricultural area economies. With the onset of Soviet rule, parts of today's oblast formed part of the neighbouring Poltava, Chernihiv and Kharkiv oblasts. However, in 1939, the Sumy oblast was created, the boundaries of which have remained stable ever since.

Although this area was absorbed into the Russian Empire at around the same time as much of the eastern parts of Ukraine, including Kharkiv and Luhans'k, the political orientation of the area has always been different. For example, in the regions to the south in Luhans'k and Donets'k in the Donbas, the existence of minerals had led to their rapid industrialisation and the influx of migrants from Russia to fill the workplaces in the factories and coalmines. In contrast, Sumy kept its predominantly rural character. The urban areas were small, often having a mixed Ukrainian, Russian and Jewish population.

Studies, at the University of Glamorgan, entitled, 'Crossing Borders: History, Theories and Identities, December 2-4 2004.

134   Information regarding Sumy can be found at http://online.sumy.ua/eng/history/index.html, accessed 3 May 2004.

Such differences are manifested in the statistics regarding the language of instruction in schools in the post-war years. In contrast to the very low proportion of children being taught in Ukrainian by the mid 1980s in Kharkiv and especially Luhans'k, in Sumy, even after decades of 'russification' pressure from the centre, the figure was still 49.7 percent.[135]

Turning to election results since 1991, the oblast has until post-2004, supported left wing forces in all the elections. However, a distinction here needs to be made. Whilst in Luhans'k it was noted how the 'hard left' policies of the KPU were popular, here the vote has been more diversified across a range of leftist forces. For example, in the 1998 parliamentary elections, whilst 25.43 percent voted for KPU, the Progressive Socialists also gained 20.89 percent and the Socialist/Peasantry Party 13.05 percent of the vote.[136] Four years later at the 2002 parliamentary elections, the results perhaps even more so depicted the area as being highly diverse in its political orientation, yet with different political parties on this occasion gaining support. The leading party here was *Nasha Ukrayina*, notably led by Viktor Yushchenko, who was born in the region, with 18.6 percent.[137] Four other parties also received significant proportions of the vote including ZYU (17.04 percent), KPU (16.49 percent), SDPU-o (15.08 percent) and Yuliya Tymoshenko's anti-presidential party gaining 7.5 percent. These results indeed demonstrate that cumulatively whilst around a quarter of the votes went to Yushchenko and Tymoshenko, who both advocated political and economic reforms, in contrast over 30 percent voted for the pro-presidential oligarchic 'parties of power' and maintenance of the *status-quo.*

In more recent elections, one can also depict the unique nature of voting patterns in Sumy oblast. In the 2004 Presidential elections, Yushchenko gained an impressive 79.5 percent of all votes, which is in stark contrast to the 25 percent he gained in Kharkiv and his total rejection in Luhans'k. Such a result can be explained first by the fact that Yushchenko was actually born in Sumy oblast and thus gained much support as being 'our man' or 'one of us' in this area. However, no less importantly, some of the central tenets of

---

135   Arel, D., "Language Politics in Independent Ukraine: Towards One or Two State Languages?", 597-622.
136   Craumer, P.R. and Clem, J.I., "Ukraine's emerging Electoral Geography", 18.
137   http://www.cvk.ukrpack.net, accessed 7 August 2002.

Yushchenko's presidential campaign, such as development of the Ukrainian countryside and support for cultural and linguistic ukrainisation, would have been embraced far more easily in rural Sumy oblast than in the more russified and sovietised Kharkiv and Luhans'k oblasts. Again, in the 2006 and 2007 Parliamentary elections, whilst the Party of the Regions, seeing itself as the protector of the interests of 'Eastern Ukraine' gained strong support across Luhans'k and Kharkiv oblasts, in Sumy, it polled only 10.92 and 15.69 per cent. In contrast, the parties of BYUT and *Nasha Ukrayina* added together gained over 52 percent in 2006 and up to 65 percent in 2007.

Finally, regarding the national profile of the area and language use, figures from the 2001 census demonstrate that Ukrainians comprise 88.8 percent of the population, an increase of 3.3 percent since 1989 and Russians 9.4 percent, a decrease of 3.9 percent.[138] Turning to language use, 92.4 percent of Ukrainians view Ukrainian as their native language, whilst intriguingly only 89.6 percent of Russians view Russian as their native language. The remainder, 10.4 percent, sees Ukrainian as their native language. Such figures therefore, if taken in direct comparison with those of the other two study areas, indicate that Sumy has a far higher ethnic Ukrainian population, which is in the vast majority, Ukrainian-speaking. In contrast, the Russian influence here, certainly in terms of population and language use, is far less. Indeed, the 10.4 percent of Ukrainophone Russians perhaps demonstrates the dominance of Ukrainian in the local environment, a fact certainly confirmed by the hegemony of Ukrainian language signs and advertising around the city of Sumy (see Plate 2.3).

Such findings are confirmed by the changes, which have been occurring in the education system. The figures clearly demonstrate that the state-sponsored linguistic ukrainisation is being embraced in this area, with the proportion of children learning in Ukrainian jumping from 46.1 percent in 1991/2 to 83 percent in 2000/1.[139] (see Tables 2.4 and 2.6). Also in the area of pre-school education, by 2000 97.7 percent of children were taught in the Ukrainian language, a figure higher than the proportion of Ukrainians in the local population (see Tables 2.3 and 2.5). Overall, such results point to the

---

138   www.ukrcensus.gov.ua, accessed 29 April 2004.
139   "Systema osvity v Ukrayini: stan ta perspectyvy rosvytku", 8.

fact that Sumy differs greatly from the simplistic 'west-east' image of Ukraine, with eastern areas seen as politically pro-Russian and Russian speaking areas. Whilst Sumy is a border area, and as a result of this had throughout its history long interaction with Russians and Russian culture, nevertheless the area owing to its lack of mineral resources was never highly industrialised and 'russified'. As such, today the area has a very different socio-political outlook than both Kharkiv and especially Luhans'k.

2.5   Conclusions

This chapter examined the significance of regionalism within the politics of identity in Ukraine. It was argued that owing to the diversity of historical legacies of many regions of modern-day Ukraine, regionalism is a far more complex phenomenon, than a simple, dichotomous 'west-east' divide. The chapter took as a point of departure an eight-region framework, which was further modified to create a framework of ten regions. Concepts such as 'Western Ukraine' were found to fail to take into account the contrasting historical, demographic and economic profiles of the lands, which comprise the historical regions of Galicia, Volhynia, Transcarpathia and Bykovyna. Furthermore, in an effort to illuminate the inherent nuances and subtleties within and between regions in Ukraine, this chapter aimed to deconstruct the concept of 'Eastern Ukraine' as a unitary, homogenous space. In particular, three study areas, all adjacent to the Russian-Ukrainian border, were chosen as sites for a local, comparative study. From a brief analysis of these three study areas, significant variations were found to exist, notably in their varied responses to the state-led linguistic ukrainisation project since 1991. These initial findings, however, must be placed under empirical scrutiny, which is the focus for Chapters 3 and 4.

Table 2.1 **Result of the final round of the 2004 Ukrainian Presidential elections, dated 26 December 2004, in the three study areas (percentage of votes)**

Oblast	Yushchenko	Yanukovych
Luhans'k	6.2	91.2
Kharkiv	26.4	68.1
Sumy	79.5	16.9

Source: www.cvk.gov.ua, accessed 15 October 2007.

Table 2.2 **Results of the 2006 and 2007 Ukrainian Parliamentary elections in the three study areas (percentage of vote)**

	2006			2007		
Oblast	Party of the Regions	BYUT	Nasha Ukrayina	Party of the Regions	BYUT	Nasha Ukrayina/ Narodna Samoboronna
Luhans'k	74.3	3.7	2	73.6	5.1	1.73
Kharkiv	51.7	12.7	5.9	49.6	16.4	8.1
Sumy	10.9	33.3	19.4	15.7	44.5	20.7

Source: www.cvk.gov.ua, accessed 15 October 2007.

Table 2.3 **Language of instruction in pre-school education establish-ments in the three study areas 2000/1**

Oblasts	% Ukrainian	% Russian
Luhans'k	19.7	80.3
Kharkiv	82.7	17.3
Sumy	97.7	2.3

Source: "Sistema osviti v Ukrayini: stan ta perspectivi rosvitku", in *National'na bespeka i oborona*, no. 4, 28, 2002: 5.

Table 2.4 **The Language of instruction in education establishments in the three study areas 2000/1**

Oblasts	% Ukrainian	% Russian
Luhans'k	17	83
Kharkiv	55	45
Sumy	83	17

Source: "Sistema osviti v Ukrayini: stan ta perspectivi rosvitku", in *National'na bespeka i oborona*, no. 4, 28, 2002: 5.

Table 2.5 Language of instruction in pre-school education establishments in Ukraine 2000/1

Oblasts	% Ukrainian	% Russian
Autonomous Republic of Crimea	2.8	96.3
The City of Sevastopol	1.6	98.4
Cherkas'ka	99.1	0.1
Chernihivs'ka	99.5	0.5
Chernivets'ka	93.6	0.2
Dnipropetrovs'ka	84.5	15.5
Donets'ka	34.5	65.5
Ivano-Frankivs'ka	100	0
Kharkivs'ka	**82.7**	**17.3**
Kheml'nyts'ka	99.9	0.1
Khersons'ka	83.2	16.8
Kirovohrads'ka	98.2	1.8
Kyivs'ka	99.6	0.4
L'vivs'ka	99.7	0
Luhans'ka	**19.7**	**80.3**
Mykolaivs'ka	90.4	9.6
Odes'ka	62.9	35.4
Poltavs'ka	98.3	1.7
Rivens'ka	99.9	0.1
Sums'ka	**97.7**	**2.3**
Ternopil's'ka	100	0
Vynnyts'ka	100	0
Zakarpats'ka	90.2	0.6
Zaporiz'ka	62.9	37.1
Zhytomyrs'ka	99.8	0.2

Source: "Sistema osviti v Ukrayini: stan ta perspectivi rosvitku", in *National'na bespeka i oborona*, no. 4, 28, 2002: 5.

Table 2.6 **Language of instruction in education establishments in Ukraine 2000/1**

Oblasts	% Ukrainian	% Russian
Autonomous Republic of Crimea	0.9	97
The City of Sevastopol	2.0	98
Cherkas'ka	96	4
Chernihivs'ka	94	6
Chernivets'ka	81	2
Dnipropetrovs'ka	68	32
Donets'ka	14	86
Ivano-Frankivs'ka	99	1
Kharkivs'ka	**55**	**45**
Kheml'nyts'ka	98	2
Khersons'ka	76	24
Kirovohrads'ka	89	11
Kyivs'ka	97	3
L'vivs'ka	98	2
Luhans'ka	**17**	**83**
Mykolaivs'ka	74	26
Odes'ka	47	51
Poltavs'ka	93	7
Rivens'ka	99.7	0.3
Sums'ka	**83**	**17**
Ternopil's'ka	99.7	0.3
Vynnyts'ka	97	2
Zakarpats'ka	86	2
Zaporiz'ka	45	55
Zhytomyrs'ka	96	4

Source: "Sistema osviti v Ukrayini: stan ta perspectivi rosvitku", in *National'na bespeka i oborona*, no.4, 28, 2002: 8.

Plate 2: Banner hanging across the main thoroughfare in central Kharkiv, *Sumskaya,* with a quotation by President Leonid Kuchma, *"It is possible to call Kharkiv the capital of Ukrainian-Russian co-operation".*

(Photographed by P. W. Rodgers, March 2003)

Plate 3   **Banner, in Ukrainian language, in the central square in Sumy,**
"The Sumy region - our motherland, Ukraine - our Mother-
land"

(Photographed by P. W. Rodgers, April 2003)

3 Contesting History: State Narratives of the Nation

The first step in liquidating a people is to erase its memory. Destroy its books, its culture, and its history. Then have somebody write new books, invent a new history. Before long, the nation will begin to forget what it is and what it was. The world around it will forget even faster.

- Milan Kundera

This chapter examines how the Ukrainian state uses history textbooks as 'tools' to introduce schoolchildren to key historical episodes around which a modern Ukrainian national identity could be shaped. Attempts to 'historicise' Ukrainian national identity must answer fundamental questions; Who are we? Where have we come from? Where are we going? Who are we not? The final question is pertinent. A key part of understanding 'who you are' is the ability to distinguish from others.

Since 1991, new Ukrainian history textbooks have emerged and there has been a subsequent expansion of academic study within this area.[140] This study aims to complement these works in a number of ways. To increase our understanding, three questions are posed:

- Since gaining independence, has there been a 'crystallisation' of a single state-sponsored historical narrative?
- To what degree Russia is presented as a distinct, 'other'?
- Is there a standardisation of history textbooks used in schools across Ukraine or are there any regional variations?

---

140   See the contributions in the above, *Ukrayins'ka Dydaktyka*. In the English language, please refer to two studies; Janmaat, J.G., *Nation-Building in Post-Soviet Ukraine: Educational Policy and the Response of the Russian-Speaking Population*, University of Amsterdam, Netherlands Geographical Society, 2000, especially chapter 4 and Popson, N., "The Ukrainian History Textbook", 2001.

3.1   Teaching the Ukrainian past

Textbooks are a key educational 'tool' through which the desired values
and norms of a political system are presented to young members of society.
Venezky argues that the contents of textbooks can be divided into a "manifest
curriculum", which provides raw facts and figures and the "latent curriculum",
which aims to instil certain social and political understandings in the recipients.[141] This comes in the form of "a series of secondary messages, transmitted on top of the manifest curriculum through omission and commission."[142]
Thus, textbooks provide an ideal method to examine if and how the state has
attempted to weave a national historical narrative. The existing literature on
the use of textbooks by states to forge collective identities is varied and wide-
ranging, and has expanded with the emergence of new states with the
collapse of communism across Europe.[143] In particular, trends in academic
study have found the necessity for states to 'populise' history for schoolchildren, for each nation to have one or several 'glorious' moments in their
history and more generally, the concept of the nation. For example, Solonari
studied to what extent history textbooks depicted Moldova as a separate
nation or a part of a wider Romanian nation, formed by external Russian
power.[144] Matzung explores how the contemporary German state is attempting to interpret the socialist past within German history, being careful to
provide a narrative, which is not too much at odds with popular memories of
the period.[145]

To understand present realities in Ukraine, it is imperative to recognise
how recent changes have arisen. In the 1980s, the Soviet authorities only

---

141   Venezky, R., "Textbooks in School and Society", in Jackson, P.W., (ed.), *Handbook
of Research and Curriculum*, New York: MacMillan, 1992: 438.
142   *Ibid.*, 438.
143   Interested readers may note that the Georg Eckert Institute in Braunsweig
(Germany) is dedicated to the study of textbooks. An international seminar was held
there in 1999, with participants from Germany, Lithuania, Belarus, Ukraine,
Moldova, Georgia and Azerbaijan. Many of the papers can be found in the Ukrainian language in *Ukrains'ka Istorychna Dydaktyka*.
144   Solonari, V., "Narrative, Identity, State: History Teaching in Moldova", in *East
European Politics and Societies*, 16, 2, 2002: 414-445.
145   Matzing, H.C., "Sotsialystychnye minulye v nimets'kix pidruchnikax – do pytannya
pro vivchennya neprostoi temi", in *Ukrayins'ka Istorychna Dydaktyka*, 291-307.

allowed 'History of Ukraine' to be an 'additional' subject, *istorychnye krayezhnavstvo*, (the history of a 'region'). However, in light of continuing calls for a reappraisal of historical events in the late 1980s, the incumbent Ukrainian Communist leadership was forced to take note. In October 1988, the first secretary Shcherbytskyi called for an improvement in the teaching of history.[146] Following this a programme was initiated to develop historical research in Ukraine, which by 1989/1990, had led to a single 'History of Ukraine' course being introduced into schools across Soviet Ukraine. This course began to be taught in parallel with the 'History of the USSR' course.[147] Also, the name of the publishing house was transformed from *Radyans'ka Shkola* (The Soviet School) to *Osvita* (Education). From 1991/2, the Ministry of Education in independent Ukraine radically changed the structure of historical education, bringing in two separate subjects, 'History of Ukraine' and 'World History' to be taught in a parallel and synchronised fashion. The clear understanding of the new state elites of the importance of education in the projects of Ukrainian nation and state building were summed up by Anatoly Pohribny, the deputy education minister under Kravchuk between 1992-1994 when he stated, "Education should be directly subordinated to the demands of building an independent Ukrainian state."[148] By the middle of the 1990s, the publishing house *Osvita*, which continued to produce textbooks by historians working at the Institute of Ukrainian History, was joined by a second publishing house, *Geneza,* although its publications were still predominantly based on the work of the same historians. By the year 2000, numerous other publishing houses, based in cities across Ukraine, had begun to publish 'History of Ukraine' textbooks.

However, the education system, despite such developments, remains highly centralised. The Ministry of Education produces programmes and guidelines to which schools and teachers must adhere. The textbooks used in

---

146 For a detailed overview of this period, see Stanislav Kulchytskyi's comments in the seminar, "Vitchiznyana Istoriya v shkolax i vuzax Ukrayiny: Ostannye Desyatyrychchya", Kiev: Kennan Institute, 2002: 3-13.

147 For a detailed comparison of the Soviet Ukrainian textbooks and the later textbooks used in independent Ukraine, see Janmaat, J.G, *Nation-Building in Post-Soviet Ukraine*: Chapter 4.

148 Quoted in Wilson, A., *Ukrainian Nationalism in the 1990s: A Minority faith*, 157.

schools must be 'recommended' by the Ministry.[149] Also the education system and the teaching of separate subjects, such as history, must adhere to the 'National Doctrine of Educational Development', which introduces the state project, 'Education: Ukraine in the twenty-first century'.[150] Within the national doctrine, it is stated how the state should ensure:

> The preservation and enrichment of Ukrainian cultural and historical traditions, culti-vation of a respectful attitude to national sacred objects, the Ukrainian language, history and culture of Ukraine's rooted peoples and national minorities, and forma-tion of inter-ethnic and interpersonal relations.[151]

Importantly, therefore, all history textbooks before being utilised in schools across Ukraine, must be accredited. This is done by Ukraine's Ministry of Education which works to this end in conjunction with the Ukrain-ian Academy of Sciences. The following section specifically focuses on how such proclamations are interpreted and presented in history textbooks.

3.2   Narrating the 'History of Ukraine'

Textbooks used for analysis are all on the Ministry of Education's rec-ommended list and cover Grades 7, 8, 9, 10 and 11 of the Ukrainian educa-tional system.

Grade 7: Ladichenko, T.V., Sviderskaya., V.V., Sviderskiy, Y.Y., *Istoriia Ukrayiny; 7 klas*, Zaporozh'ye: Prem'er, 2002.

Grade 8: Vlasov, V.S., *Istoriia Ukrayiny: 8 klas*, Kiev: "A.S.K", 2002.

Grade 9: Turchenko, F.H., Moroko, V.N., *Istoriia Ukrayiny: konets XVIII-nachalo XX veka*, Kiev: Geneza, 2001.

---

149   See, *Kalendarno-tematichne planuvannya z Istoriyi Ukrayini, Vsesvitnyoi Istoriyi, Pravozhavstva, za novymy (2001 roku) navchal'nymy prohramamy*, Prem'er, Zaporizhzhya, 2001.

150   For confirmation of this, see "Pro Natsional'nu doktrynu rozvytku osvity", No.347, 17 April, 2002, which can be found at, www.kuchma.gov.ua/main/?whatto-557, ac-cessed 1 March 2005.

151   *Ibid.*, 36.

Grade 10: Danilenko, V.M., Husenkov, S.H., Kolodyazhnyi, N.N., *Istoriia Ukrayiny: 10 klas,* Zaporozh'ye: Prem'er, 2002.
Grade 11: Shevchuk, V.P., Taranenko, N.G., Levitas, F.,L., Gisem, A.V., *Istoriia Ukrayiny: 11 klas,* Zaporozh'ye: Prem'er, 2001.

For each of the grades, there is a selection of textbooks available for individual teachers and schools to use. An interesting development in recent years has been the emergence of the *Prem'er* publishing house based in Zaporizhzhiya. While textbooks published in Kiev by *Geneza,* A.S.K and *Osvita,* are all printed solely in the Ukrainian language, *Prem'er* publishes in both the Ukrainian and Russian languages. Therefore, the author chose to use a variety of textbooks, from different publishing houses, in an effort to determine any emerging *regional* variations in the historical narrative.

The analysis focuses on the (re)interpretation of significant events, personalities and periods in Russian-Ukrainian history. In Grade 7 focus is on the existence of the Kiev Rus' state. In the Grade 8 textbook, analysis concentrates on the Cossack period. Ukraine in the nineteenth century is the backdrop for the Grade 9 textbook, with special attention on how Russian-controlled Ukraine fared under the Tsars. Grades 10 and 11, turn to events of the twentieth century.

3.2.1 Grade 7 (twelve to thirteen year olds): Kiev Rus'

The legacy of Kiev Rus' plays a prominent role in the Grade 7 textbook. The authors place great emphasis on the significance of Christianity for the Ukrainian nation's development and joining to Europe in an effort to legitimate Ukraine's present day European credentials:

> The introduction of Christianity played an enormous role in the subsequent fate of the Ukrainian people. Found at the crossroads of the Christian West and the Muslim East, Kiev Rus' connected itself with Europe. Christianity introduced Rus' to a circle of European states.[152]

---

152   Ladichenko, T.V., Sviderskaya, V.V., Skiderskiy, Y.Y., *Istoria Ukrayiny: 7 klas,* 67.

However, Kiev Rus' is not seen as the first Ukrainian state. The approach is subtler arguing that Kiev Rus' was a loose amalgam of the forefathers of the East Slavic peoples, who had yet to fully develop their linguistic and cultural differences. These differences began to metamorphose following 'the collapse of Kiev Rus' into separate princedoms, accelerating the ethnic development of Ukrainian, Russian and Belarusian nationalities and facilitating the formation and strengthening of the state and their territories."[153] The text argues that the chief inheritor of the legacies of Kiev Rus' was not Muscovy, as argued by Russophile historiography, but the Galycian-Volhynian Princedom. As the text states:

> After Kiev Rus' collapsed, began a process of the political unification of lands, on which Ukrainian nationality dominated. Apart from the Princedoms, situated along the Dnipro and the Desnya (Kiev, Pereyaslav, Chernihiv, Seversk), the Halycian-Volhynian Princedom became the centre of such an association in the region surrounding the Dniester River. Statehood became the essential form of the existence of Ukrainian nationality.[154]

The ancient nature of present-day state symbols is highlighted. The text clearly states that, "the state symbols of Ukraine, the trident and the flag had their beginnings in the times of Kiev Rus' and the Galycian-Volhynian state" and explains how the trident came to be an emblem of the Ukrainian People's Republic in 1918 and finally was confirmed as a national symbol of Ukraine in the constitution in 1996.[155] Thus the authors point out, 'In this way, our national symbols reflect the historical traditions and beliefs of the Ukrainian people'.[156] In its concluding remarks, the text reiterates the importance of Kiev Rus' for understanding the genesis of the Ukrainian nation and state, using the words of Hrushevskyi:

> In the period of Kiev Rus', [Ukrainian nationality] received a powerful stimulus for its political, economic, cultural and ethnic development. The well-known Ukrainian historian Mykhailo Hrushevskyi wrote, "Kiev Rus' is the first form of Ukrainian state-

---

153   *Ibid.*, 109.
154   *Ibid.*, 110.
155   Ladichenko, T.V., Sviderskaya, V.V., Skiderskiy, Y.Y., *Istoria Ukrayiny: 7 klas,* 111.
156   *Ibid.*, 111.

hood." In modern historiography there are different evaluations, but all historians agree that the roots of the Ukrainian people come from Kiev Rus'.[157]

Overall, this textbook provides an interpretation of Kiev Rus', which does not give Ukrainians full ownership of Kiev Rus'. Nonetheless, ample material highlights the historical importance of the period for today's Ukrainian nation and state. Interestingly, this book places great emphasis on the continuity between Kiev Rus' and the Galycian-Volhynian Princedom. This linkage is not apparent in the textbook analysed by Janmaat.[158] This leads one to conclude that the state has grounded its beliefs of this period on those developed by Hrushevskyi.

3.2.2 Grade 8 (thirteen to fourteen year olds): The Cossack period

The Grade 8 textbook idealises the Cossack period as a time when the Ukrainian people struggled for their right for an independent state:

> Thus, the appearance of a new layer of Ukrainian society – Cossackdom, gave evidence of the enormous ability of our ancestors in life...The Cossacks grew stronger, ably defended their native land from foreigners so as to uphold the ethnic distinctiveness and also to create one's own state...The colonisation of the land was the result of the economic activity of the Cossack, and consequently, widened the living space of the Ukrainian people, which occurred peacefully, without the conquering of foreign territories.[159]

Cossacks are introduced as a 'peaceful' people who had no desire to conquer others' lands. This theme is held in sharp contrast to their neighbours, the Poles, the Turks and the Russians, portrayed as warring peoples, ever eager to grab more land. The Cossacks are explicitly seen as the forefathers of the Ukrainian nation - "the input of the Cossacks into the culture and history of Ukraine is heavy, which is why now Ukrainians are called the 'Cossack people'."[160] The linear nature of the history of Ukrainian statehood focuses on the Cossack state, the Zaporizhzhian Sich'. This is seen as a state, in which many traditions of the 'Ukrainian' proto-state of

---

157 Ibid., 119.
157 See Janmaat, J.G., Nation-Building in Post-Soviet Ukraine, ch. 4.
158 Ibid.
159 Vlasov, V.S., Istoriia Ukrayiny: 8 klas, Kiev: A.S.K, 2002: 31.

Galycian-Volynian princedom are represented. The text also highlights the democratic and law-abiding nature of the Ukrainian people:

> The Zaporizhzhian Sich' played an exceptionally important role in the history of the Ukrainian people…It was, as academics note, an intermediary link between the Ha-lycian-Volynian Kingdom and the Ukrainian separate Cossack republic under the Hetman, Bohdan Khmelnytsk'yi…In the Sich' was formed their own organs of power and the powers of the government and a legal system. It was a Christian Cossack republic, one of the first republics in Europe at that time.[161]

The text introduces the 'national-liberation war' of the Ukrainian people against the Polish state, *Rzeczpospolita* (1648-1658), a war seen as 'just' for the Ukrainians' rightful gaining of state independence. Using the term 'regeneration', readers are left in no doubt that some sort of Ukrainian statehood existed previously. The link is made more explicit when the text tells of the Ukrainian Hetman, Khmelnytsk'yi discussing with the Poles the plight of his people in 1649:

> In discussion with the Polish envoys, it was clearly outlined the right of the Ukrain-ian people for the creation of their own state in its ethnic borders. Concerning this point, (Khmelnytskyi) underlined that the Ukrainian Cossack state was a successor of Kiev Rus'.[162]

The text provides a subtle account of the 1654 Treaty of Pereiaslav. Whilst it is argued that Khmelnytsk'yi signed the union with Muscovy because he had no choice, the text makes explicit that not all of Ukraine was suppor-tive of this stance. The text quotes a Ukrainian noble, who stated, "I see the misfortune, that Khmelnytsk'yi betrayed us all unintentionally to the Muscovite Tsar."[163] This illustrates the more nationalistically orientated view that Khmelnytsk'yi, under no circumstances, can be viewed as a hero for the Ukrainian people. He made the cardinal sin of joining up with Muscovy.[164]

---

160 *Ibid.*, 31.
161 *Ibid.*, 40.
162 Vlasov, V.S., *Istoriia Ukrayiny: 8 klas*, 121.
163 *Ibid.*, 147.
164 For an excellent discussion of the different viewpoints on this complex issue, see Plokhy, S., "The Ghosts of Pereyaslav: Russo-Ukrainian Historical Debates in the Post-Soviet Era", in *Europe-Asia Studies,* 53, 3, 2001: 489-505.

However, the text soon refers back to the line, used in previous post-Soviet Ukrainian textbooks about Khmelnytsk'yi being a genuine Ukrainian hero:

> Bohdan Khmelnytsk'yi is one of the brightest figures of Ukrainian history...the main achievement of Khmelnytsk'yi was the regeneration of the Ukrainian state. The results of the national-liberation war, headed by the Hetman are regarded as the restoration of an independent state, which united all the Ukrainian lands and would become an inheritor of Kiev Rus'.[165]

Russia as an 'other' is also introduced. The real problem of the Pereiaslav Treaty is explained as the Tsar who, when entering into the 'union', had very different intentions from those of the Cossacks. Here begins a narrative of Tsarist Muscovy 'tricking' the Ukrainians to join them and then using their wealth for the needs of the Muscovite Empire. Furthermore, the text introduces a table of comparison between the Cossack Ukrainian state and Muscovy (see Table 3.1).[166]

Pupils analyse the table and answer the questions: Was there any possibility of an equal union between Ukraine and Muscovy? Did Ukraine have a perspective for her own development in a union with Muscovy? As the table clearly demonstrates, the author is attempting to strengthen the claim that Muscovy is an alien 'other' for Ukrainians for a whole host of reasons. The table provides a clear explanation from two perspectives. One view could be that the Ukrainians were unable to develop on their own accord under the Tsars. On the other side, it could explain why a 'backward' Muscovy had to 'colonise' Ukraine for its own purposes, as this was the only way possible to control the more 'progressive' Ukraine. The table thus gives the reader a clear lead-in to the subsequent sections, regarding the forced 'russification' of Ukraine and the continual degradation of elements of Ukrainian statehood.

---

165   Vlasov, V.S., *Istoriia Ukrayiny: 8 klas*, 153.
166   *Ibid.*, 155.

Table 3.1 **Comparison between the Hetmanate Ukraine state and Muscovy**

Hetmanate Ukraine	*Muscovy*
1. Republic	1. Absolute monarchy
2. Feudal land ownership and serfdom abolished. Developing Cossack land ownership on the basis of freely hired labour.	2. Basis of economic order – feudal land ownership and serfdom.
3. City self-rule.	3. Cities without self-rule.
4. Free relations with the entire cultural world. Aspiration towards European education, strong tendencies to gain freedom of speech, thought, printing.	4. Culture contained features of being closed and stern, full of non-recognition of anything foreign. Great religious fanaticism, impatience to foreign beliefs.
5. Influence of Western Europe culture in the areas of rights, science and education.	5. Almost devoid of any cultural links with Western Europe.

The final area of interest in the Grade 8 textbook concerns Ivan Mazepa. Whilst in Russophile and Soviet historiography, the 'treachery' of Mazepa is witnessed in his betrayal of the Tsar; here a profoundly different version of events is given.[167] He is represented as a Ukrainian hero who attempted to improve the lot of his fellow countrymen by whatever means possible:

> The aspiration of Mazepa to create one's own elite, his far-sighted policy in the sphere of culture and education provided another 80 years existence of the Hetmanate state. It influenced the future development of the Ukrainian people and her state traditions and the formation of a national culture. The epoch of Mazepa – is a time of the regeneration of Ukraine, an epoch of her political, economic and cultural progress.[168]

The Swedish king's approach to Muscovy across Ukraine to fight the Tsar, Peter the First, at the battle of Poltava in 1709, is said to have "compelled Mazepa to decisive actions for the liberation of Hetmanshchyna."[169] Mazepa's actions are justified for the greater good of protecting his own state. The concluding remarks of the text uphold the narrative of Mazepa as a national hero.

Overall, the Grade 8 textbook idealises the Cossack state as a direct successor of Kiev Rus', which provides a key part of the linear history of Ukrainian statehood. The text demonstrates virtues of the Ukrainian people: peace-loving, democratic and law-abiding, in spite of having to live in terrible conditions, forever 'struggling' for their right for an independent state. Such virtues are held in direct contrast to Ukraine's neighbours who are vilified as warring peoples, forever intent to capture 'foreign' lands from the Ukrainian people. The harsh policies of Tsarist Muscovy towards Ukraine are particularly criticised, which only highlights the fundamental 'otherness' of Muscovy in its cultural and political traditions. Post-Soviet Ukrainian textbooks adopt several differences in their portrayal of two controversial figures, Khmelnytsk'yi and Mazepa, while retaining some similarities. Khmelnytsk'yi is

---

167   Janmaat, J.G., *Nation-Building in Post-Soviet Ukraine*, ch. 4.
168   Vlasov, V.S., *Istoriia Ukrayiny: 8 klas*, 212.
169   *Ibid.*, 216.

depicted as a national hero who had no choice in signing the Treaty with Muscovy in 1654, following the trends found in previously analysed textbooks. Whereas, the portrayal of Mazepa is far more enthusiastic.

3.2.3 Grade 9 (fourteen to fifteen year olds): Ukraine in the nineteenth century

This textbook concentrates on how Ukraine, divided into two parts, under Austro-Hungarian rule and under Russian Tsarist rule, fared through the nineteenth century. Here the focus will be on Russian-controlled Ukraine.

- Is the assimilation of large segments of Ukraine's population into the ruling Russian culture viewed as voluntary and natural, or is it portrayed as forcibly imposed?

- Was the linguistic russification, a result of an imperial policy aimed to denationalise Ukrainians, or did it occur organically through the interaction of Ukrainians and Russians over time?

The Turchenko and Moroko clearly indicate in the introduction that the book continues the story of the teleological triumph of the Ukrainian people in their struggle for national self-determination:

> The downtrodden, illiterate Ukrainian population was transformed into the Ukrainian nation with all those features, which characterise other European societies. And this took place in conditions when the Ukrainians with all possible means were forced to forget their past; there were attempts to rid any feelings of being Ukrainian. However, it was in vain. Not by accident, namely in the nineteenth century, was born the Ukrainian national hymn, "Ukraine has not perished yet"... In the beginning of the twentieth century, the Ukrainian people created political parties and began an open struggle for the regeneration of her state. Without this struggle, without the intense search for their Ukrainian way in history, there would not be a modern Ukrainian state.[170]

---

170   Turchenko, F.H., Moroko, V.N., *Istoriia Ukrayiny: konets XVIII – nachalo XX veka*, Kiev: Geneza, 2001: 3-4.

The Tsarist regime is portrayed repeatedly as an evil empire, using Ukraine for her own personal ends, irrespective of the needs of the Ukrainian people. Concerning the education system in Ukraine the authors make clear that:

> The Tsarist government planted in Ukraine such a system of education which was summoned to satisfy the demands of the state and simultaneously helped to extinguish in Ukrainian people their national consciousness, fasten a feeling of inadequacy, create the impression of the leading role of the 'Russian nation' in the life of Ukraine.[171]

In particular the text draws attention to the russification of southern and eastern Ukraine, arguing that the Tsarist regime used the incoming Russian migrants as 'tools' in their battle with the Ukrainian national movement. The text makes a clear judgement that the Russian language was 'imposed' onto all Ukrainian lands by imperial and colonial means and certainly did not emerge as a result of the natural interaction of Russians and Ukrainians.

Whilst large parts of the text focus on the negativity of the Tsarist regime and the consequences of its actions in Ukraine, the text also concentrates on the reaction of Ukrainians, showing a 'national revival' slowing emerging. The text recalls the Cyrylo-Methodius Brotherhood of Ukrainian intellectuals, founded in the 1840s, which was set up to fight for the rights of the Ukrainian people:

> The great achievement of the Ukrainian national-liberation movement of the first half of the nineteenth century was the organisation and activity of the Cyrylo-Methodius brotherhood. This national, patriotic organisation grew in the traditions of Ukrainian socio-political movements of previous generations and opened a new stage in the struggle of the Ukrainian people for their national and social liberation.[172]

The text concentrates on the teleological struggle of the Ukrainian people to fight foreign interference and uphold their right for national self-

---

171   *Ibid.*, 108.
172   Turchenko, F.H., Moroko, V.N., *Istoriia Ukrayiny*, 66.

determination. The reader is left in no doubt that russification was imposed on the population of Ukraine by state-led migration, educational and cultural policies of the Tsarist 'other' regime. With the concentration on the plight of ethnic Ukrainians comes a simultaneous omission of the role of other ethnic groups, namely Russians, Jews, Poles in the history of this period.

3.2.4   Grade 10 (fifteen to sixteen year olds): Ukraine in the twentieth century: 1915-1939

The Grade 10 textbook focuses on the portrayal of the Ukrainian Revolution and the coming to power of the Bolsheviks in Ukraine.

- Are the Bolsheviks seen as an ideological force, which grabbed power in Russia, and subsequently Ukraine, in an attempt to forward their ideological pursuits?
- Or were the Bolsheviks essentially another form of Russian autocracy, simply dressed in different clothes?

With regard to the role of Ukraine in World War One, the text recounts how Ukrainians, forced to fight on both sides for the Austro-Hungarian Empire and the Russian Empire, finally realised that their future resided not under foreign power, but instead that the moment was right for them to seize back their rightful statehood. While attempts at establishing a Ukrainian national government are seen as drawing together the historical traditions of Ukrainian statehood, the text does not attempt to idealise them. For example, the Central Rada, the initial Ukrainian government set up in Kiev, is praised for its democratic foundations, yet criticised for being indecisive. In the uncertain climate, the text tells of how Bolshevism, with its authoritarian roots in Russia, began to assert control in Ukraine. Bolshevism is seen as a foreign imposition, which did not organically develop in Ukraine:

> The political situation in Ukraine was different from in Russia. Here the influence of the Bolsheviks was limited. Here the programme was orientated to the proletariat, among which the Ukrainians were poorly represented. The Bolsheviks viewed the Ukrainian national movement with hostility. This is explained by the fact that the

Bolsheviks in general were represented by Russians and by the russified proletariat.[173]

While there is some admission of support from within Ukraine, these people are seen to have only supported the Bolsheviks because they had been forcibly 'russified'. However, while Bolshevism is seen as a foreign force, inherently related to the Russian 'other', there is an admission of the Party's ideological beliefs. Again, the subsequent failure of the Central Rada to hold onto power is explained not simplistically as Ukraine being seized by the marauding Bolsheviks from Russia. Instead it is seen to have occurred as a combination of the indecisiveness of the Ukrainian leadership, the passivity of the population and the astute political eye of the Bolshevik power. The text strives to present the new Soviet power in Ukraine as an extension of former Russian imperial power, making the implicit understanding that the USSR, as a union of equal republics, was a sham right from the onset. As the text states:

> The insertion of the UkrSSR into the configuration of the USSR – a single, multinational state with strong central power, orientated in the interests of Russia - for many decades placed the fate of the Ukrainian people in a state of dependence on the policy of the Union leadership.[174]

On the other hand, the text argues that the creation of the UkrSSR should not be viewed as a one-dimensional, puppet state completely controlled by Russia. Although attempts to create an independent Ukrainian state had failed, Ukrainians still exhibited much autonomy from Russia. As the text states:

> The legal position of the UkrSSR at the beginning of the 1920s was formally an independent state according to the Constitution of 1919. The official independence of Ukraine was a concession of the Bolsheviks to the Ukrainian national movement.

---

173   Danilenko, V.M., Husenkov, S.H., Kolodyazhnyi, N.N., *Istoriia Ukrayiny: 10 klas, Zaporozh'ye, Prem'er*, 39.

174   Danilenko, V.M., Husenkov, S.H., Kolodyazhnyi, N.N., *Istoriia Ukrayiny*, 144.

Without the Ukrainian revolution and the national state of 1917-1919, there would have been no Soviet Ukrainian state.[175]

In such a fashion, the text cleverly incorporates these events into the wider scheme of Ukraine's history. The importance of gaining recognition as a 'national republic' within the configuration of the USSR for Ukraine is emphasised:

> However the proclamation of the USSR strengthened several gains of the Ukrainian people. The territorial integrity of Ukraine was recognised and Ukraine had its own administrative apparatus...The Ukrainian Socialist Soviet Republic became a clearly defined national and territorial whole with its own administrative centre and apparatus. In such a way, Ukrainians in the end gained the territorial-administrative frameworks, which reflected their national distinctiveness, that is to say, which they had been without since the time of the Cossack Hetmanate of the eighteenth century.[176]

The remaining sections deal with the famine of 1921 and the subsequent Great Famine of 1932/3. The text endeavours to highlight that one of main reasons for the tragedies was the lack of real Ukrainian statehood. In both cases, the text aims to make clear that the Ukrainian leadership did turn to the central Soviet leadership for assistance when people began to perish in large numbers. This is an effort to elaborate on the consequences and dangers of being dependant on foreign 'others'. Concerning the key debate, whether the Great Famine of 1932/3 was due to policy devised by central Soviet leadership explicitly against the Ukrainian people or simply part of the ideological battle to gain support for their collectivisation drive, the authors fail to demonstrate full support for either view. The text states that the famine of 1921 "was the first time famine was applied as a method of state power", thus making an implicit understanding that the subsequent famine of 1932/3 was the second, more highly orchestrated attempt.[177] Similarly, the text omits any reference to the fact that members of nationalities other than Ukrainians also

---

175   *Ibid.*, 138.
176   *Ibid.*, 143.
177   Danilenko, V.M., Husenkov, S.H., Kolodyazhnyi, N.N., *Istoriia Ukrayiny*, 130.

died from starvation in Ukraine. Yet, the text does remain, on the whole, impartial:

> The Ukrainian people have lived through many tragedies, but the history of Ukraine does not know anything more destructive than the Great Famine of the 1930s. The reasons for it are as yet still not totally clear. Some consider that the famine was planned by Stalin and his comrades earlier in order to destroy the Ukrainian peasantry, which was seen as the stronghold of nationalism and private-ownership psychology. Others prove that (the famine) was the consequence of a thoughtless policy to acquire means for industrialisation, in which no attention was paid to the fate of the peasantry. One thing is evident – the famine in Ukraine arose not as a result of drought, but was organised artificially.[178]

Also, the text recognises that the famine occurred in other agricultural regions of the USSR, although Ukraine was hardest hit. In general, blame is apportioned to the Stalinist high leadership with the Great Famine seen as "the most horrific of the many crimes of Stalinism."[179]

This textbook provides an even-handed assessment of some of the most debated parts of Ukraine's history. Although positive aspects of the Ukrainian attempts to build a state between 1917-1919 are highlighted, it does not shy away from providing a critical and measured perspective. This attempt at the regeneration of the Ukrainian state is applauded but not idealised. Whilst there are attempts to view Bolshevism and the USSR as 'foreign', the text veers away from drawing a completely negative picture. Importantly, the text emphasises how the UkrSSR, while not being the desired independent Ukrainian state, nevertheless provided the Ukrainians with a 'quasi-state' which, when the opportunity arose in 1991, became fully independent. Thus, the events of this period are interwoven into the wider historical scheme of Ukraine's statehood continually being regenerated. Similarly, with regards to the highly emotive topic of the Great Famine a relatively impartial view is maintained. The text moves away from the Soviet historiographical tradition of 'omitting' the existence of the Famine altogether. It makes clear that the Famine was artificial but restrains from claiming that it

---

178   *Ibid.*, 175.
179   Danilenko, V.M., Husenkov, S.H., Kolodyazhnyi, N.N., *Istoriia Ukrayiny*, 179.

was an act of genocide by Stalin to destroy the Ukrainian nation. Instead, the text lays the blame at the feet not of the Russian nation, but of the political system, Soviet Communism and in particular the Stalinist leadership, which is seen as an agent of an inhumane regime.

3.2.5 Grade 11 (sixteen to seventeen year olds): Ukraine and World War II

This textbook places emphasis on the period of the World War Two. Readers are constantly reminded that there was more than one resistance force to Nazi Germany's occupation of Ukraine, these being the Ukrainian Nationalists, OUN/UPA and Ukrainians loyal to the Soviet Union. The text tells how the OUN/UPA saw their role as defending their motherland: "the attack of Nazi Germany on the USSR brought hope of the restoration of Ukrainian statehood amongst participants of the OUN."[180]

However, the text however does not shy away from explicitly stating how the OUN conspired with the Nazis in the hope of reviving the Ukrainian state. The actions of the OUN are explained simply as the latest example of repressed Ukrainians trying to gain their statehood, which was obstructed by the trickery of foreign powers. Such an assessment of the OUN/UPA tries to explain their actions without attempting to glorify them. The appraisal of the Soviet Ukrainian partisans bravely fighting the Nazi occupiers is similarly neutral. The text argues that although many Ukrainians fought against the Nazis in Soviet ranks, they did so for very simple and understandable reasons. It states, "The absolute majority of the citizens of Ukraine considered that they were fighting not for the interests of the Kremlin high leadership but to defend their land from occupants."[181]

In this fashion, the actions of large numbers of Ukrainians who supported the Soviet regime are also explained. The underlying point made is that the tragedy for Ukraine was a resistance movement, split and thus severely weakened. Of particular significance is how the bloody civil war, which took place in western Ukraine in 1943-5, is interpreted. The text highlights how the previous aims of defending the homeland and the Ukrain-

---

180   Shevchuk, V.P., Taranenko, N.G., Levitas, F.L., Gisem, A.V., *Istoriia Ukrayiny: 11 klas*, Zaporozh'ye: Prem'er, 2001: 47.

181   *Ibid.*, 62.

ian nation had been cast aside for a far more cruel and irrational ideology. The text's concluding remarks regarding the War reinforce the shift in tone. The previous impartiality is reorientated to become more supportive of the role of Ukrainians fighting in Soviet ranks. The text states how over two and a half million Ukrainians fought in the Red Army, with large numbers gaining awards for their efforts, and some even becoming Heroes of the USSR. Also, the concept of the 'Great Patriotic War' is introduced together with a veiled criticism of 'nationalist' accounts of the war, which denigrate the role of Ukrainians in Soviet colours whilst glorifying the nationalist heroes of the OUN/UPA. The text clearly states:

> *Futile attempts to falsify history:* Several modern historians are making an effort to revise the character of the 'Great Patriotic War', to give it a new evaluation stating that it was only a stand for the interests of the Stalinist Empire. It is impossible to agree with this. The people defended their land from aggressors. Therefore for them the war really was *patriotic, liberating and just.* The Ukrainian soldiers for ex-ample showed the best features of character, courage, heroism, sacrificing in the name of their native land. The victory achieved in the Second World War had an in-estimable significance for the future fate of our state.[182]

In comparison with the previously analysed textbooks, this appraisal of World War Two is significantly different. It provides a less normative repre-sentation of events, including large sections concerning the OUN/UPA and also the Soviet resistance in Ukraine. Yet the narrative is itself not devoid of any underlying message. There is a concerted attempt to reassert the importance of the 'Great Patriotic War' together with an effort to steer away from a crude 'nationalist' line, which paints the OUN/UPA as the 'good guys' and the Soviets as the 'baddies'.

---

182   Shevchuk, V.P., Taranenko, N.G., Levitas, F.L., Gisem, A.V., *Istoriia Ukrayiny,* 81.

3.3 Conclusions

The textbooks concentrate on the Ukrainian ethnic nation and how its path towards national self-determination has continually been thwarted by foreign obstruction, notably Russia. However in the textbooks for the Grades 10 and 11, which deal with the still 'living' and highly contested history of the twentieth century, the narrative loses its simplistic and uni-dimensional edge. While Russia is portrayed as an external 'other' throughout, the portrayal of the USSR is far more ambiguous. Regarding World War Two, the narrative reverts to a Soviet-friendly interpretation of events.

This chapter has revealed an emerging **politics of the textbook** in Ukraine. The Ukrainian state provides a list of recommended texts, with the aim of supplying schoolchildren across Ukraine, irrespective of their place of residence, with a single historical narrative. However, in recent years there has been a rapid growth in various publishing houses, based in Kiev and elsewhere, providing alternative history textbooks. As highlighted, the textbooks published in the Zaporizhzhian based *Prem'er* publishing house, provide a far more Soviet and Russian friendly narrative of Ukraine's history. Moreover, these books are published in both the Ukrainian and Russian languages.

This situation leads one to conclude that Ukraine's inherent diversity has implicitly been allowed to flourish. However, though the state preaches the need for an all-Ukrainian textbook with one united historical narrative, rejecting previous calls for 'regional' textbooks, it seems that such interpretations are slowly emerging. In this way, some of the inherent idiosyncrasies of the Ukrainian state and nation-building projects reveal themselves. The state is publicly striving toward creating a new, revised Ukrainian historical narrative, which shifts from previous Soviet interpretations and views Russia as a foreign 'other' to Ukraine.

Simultaneously, other interpretations are also emerging, which are more closely related to previous Soviet historiography and more acceptable in Ukraine's predominantly Russian-speaking eastern regions. It is perhaps no coincidence that these textbooks are being printed in Zaporizhzhia, a large, Russian-speaking city in southeastern Ukraine. To a certain degree, this can be justified by the fact that creating a Ukrainian historical narrative, which is more 'ethnic' rather than 'civic' in nature, may alienate large segments of the Russian-speaking eastern regions, dividing rather than uniting the people. Conversely, if 'alternative' narratives are allowed to emerge, in essence the *status quo* may remain, with the state *per se* legitimating the continuation of Ukraine's present regional diversity.

4 'Where are we from?'
Negotiating 'History' in the Regions

This chapter examines how the state-sponsored historical narrative, used in school textbooks, is actually negotiated and contested at the local level. The results of qualitative in-depth interviews with school history teachers and directors are used to examine how the state narrative has actually been 'transferred' to the children. Attention focuses on to what extent the central message of the history textbooks is clearly transferred, or whether any dilution, contradictions or open avoidance of certain issues is occurring. The chapter continues with an analysis of group interviews with schoolchildren. Here, attention is placed upon how the historical narrative is 'perceived' at the local level, and to what extent such perceptions coincide with the content of the historical narrative. A thematic approach is adopted concentrating on the key issues, which arose during the fieldwork. Whilst the results from these study areas do not claim to be representative, nonetheless the means by which they may influence macro-level processes in Ukraine are analysed in the conclusions.

4.1 Linking the macro and the micro: the role of teachers in the Ukrainian classroom

Teachers were selected as a target group for this research as they occupy a key communicating link between the state-led policies outlined in history textbooks and the schoolchildren, who are seen as the 'recipients' of the information. As Piirainen states:

> It is the task of a schoolteacher to teach the coming generations to sing the national anthem and to pledge allegiance to the national flag. The past of the nation, the birth of the state, the victories and defeats in national wars, the geography of the

Fatherland, the glorious deeds of the national heroes, the genius of the national art-
ists, poets, and scientists, - all this is learnt at school.[183]

Within education studies much attention has focused on social and
cultural change and the role of teachers in such processes. For example, in
one study it is stated that, "The place of schooling in social changes continues to be problematical. We can neither decide in advance that teachers are
willing or oblivious henchmen of the social system or creators of social
change."[184] Other studies have concentrated on the inconsistencies in the
education system in which teachers are faced with 'competing imperatives'
and end up being "caught between different versions of how they ought to
act."[185] Schweisfurth, in a comparative study of the role of teachers in the
process of democratisation in Russia and South Africa, focused on how
teachers interact with the new forces of political, social and cultural
change.[186] The study highlights how teachers situated at the interface
between policy and practice "are themselves agents who, interpret, mediate
and transform policy or interfere, resist, and confound its aims, depending on
how one views the process and its outcomes."[187] Concerning changes to
history education, Schweisfurth highlights the difficulties faced by teachers in
Russia, who found the entire rejection of communism distorted the historical
perspective. According to one teacher:

There is less politics, if we can say so. The ideas and ideals of the former state,
Lenin for example, things like that. The children have new wishes, new wants. In
the former days, we tried to bring the children up in the way of Lenin. The image of
him is lost...People shouldn't now encourage us to avoid the name of Lenin because he was a part of our history. Of course, it is not so popular as it was in the old

---

183   Piirainen, P., "The Fall of an Empire, the Birth of a Nation: Perceptions of the New
      Russian National Identity", in Chulos, C.J., and Piirainen, T., *The Fall of an Empire,
      the Birth of a Nation. National Identities in Russia*, Aldershot: Ashgate, 2000: 161-
      196.
184   Berlak, A. and Berlak H., *Dilemmas of Schooling: teaching and social change*,
      London: Methuen, 1981: 134.
185   Alexander, R.J., *Versions of Primary Education*, London: Routledge, 1995: 23.
186   Schweisfurth, M., *Teachers, Democratisation and Educational Reform in Russia
      and South Africa*, Oxford: Symposium Books, 2002.
187   *Ibid.*, 10.

days, but still we are to acquaint our children with history and to tell that he was a leader of the Communist Party.[188]

In the Ukrainian context, recent research has also highlighted the inherent difficulties that teachers have in adapting to the demands of new social and political realities. This has led to protests by teachers against retraining, and ideological opposition to the curriculum changes.[189] This issue certainly arose in many of the interviews undertaken by the author, between February and April 2003, the results of which are outlined below.

Many teachers noted how previously they had taught a Soviet interpretation of history, whilst today the 'History of Ukraine' course had been specifically tailored to foster a sense of loyalty to the Ukrainian state and promote national consciousness amongst Ukraine's children. As one history teacher in Sumy remarks:

> The interpretation of various events has changed... The history of Ukraine now is directed at the creation of individual consciousness, which wasn't the case for many years. We are building a state and it is necessary to start with people, with their self-identification. There won't be a state, if we don't educate our young to be proud of their country and the fact that they are Ukrainians. Then they will do everything in their powers to develop their country.[190]

In this research, particular attention was given to this issue. For this reason, the author chose to conduct interviews with methodological specialists, working at teacher 'retraining' centres in all three study areas. In the Ukrainian education system, every teacher must spend at least one month in every five years working at the *Naukovo-metodichnyi institut bezperervnoi osviti* (Institute for uninterrupted education). As one experienced methodologist from Luhans'k, recently retired, noted:

> For teachers the previous ten years have been difficult, especially those who are middle-aged. Thus it is clear that for these people it is difficult to change the point of

---

188   Schweisfurth, M., *Teachers, Democratisation,* 73.
189   The difficulties in teacher retraining was noted in an interview with Oleg Skura-tovych, former official at the Ministry of Education, Kiev, 14 September 2000, quoted in Popson, N., "The Ukrainian History Textbook", 2001.
190   Irina, History teacher, Sumy, 19 March 2003.

view from the previous times to those of today. It is necessary to state that the text-books for History of Ukraine in the mid-1990s had a tendency towards a nationalist stance and this antagonised some teachers. The system is the same as   the pre-vious one, what needs to be taught is what the state needs to be taught. The teacher must fulfil the desire of the state. I worked at the Institute for continued edu-cation, and the teachers found this work of re-orientation very difficult. For many, it is an internal rupture.[191]

In many of the interviews, teachers expressed the difficulties they faced in teaching a new historical narrative, which 'negates' the interpretations of historical events that they had previously taught:

I think that the school programme is overweighed with details. And in the textbooks there is no overall agreed representation. Before the collapse of the USSR, there was one history, which was agreed upon by the Party forces. Now in the textbooks there is a total negation of what happened in society in those   times. There is a lot of negativity. I think that this is incorrect and unjust. For example, take the 1920s and 1930s, when our country went from being poor and agrarian to being in-dustrial and agrarian. And who did this? People, our people. Therefore, history must leave behind a footprint and a memory of these forefathers who made this history. Take again, the Second World War, on whose shoulders was the war won? On the shoulders of our people. And the post-war reconstruction? It is not fair that the feats of our people are forgotten. I in the lessons try and recall these events. Of course, there were many negative things, the Famine and the repressions, but to highlight the negatives is unjust, but unfortunately this takes place in our textbooks. Here there is an 'angry' history.[192]

Whilst there was an understanding of the need for a new historical nar-rative to move forward from previous Soviet interpretations, nevertheless, this was difficult for teachers to take on board.

---

191   Olga, former teacher training lecturer in history at Luhans'k oblast's Institute for Uninterrupted Education, 12 March 2003.
192   Timur, school history teacher, Kharkiv, 22 March 2003.

4.2   History as a Ukrainian 'political football'

Whilst many teachers understood the key role of the state in refashioning identities and the importance of a historical narrative in schools, nevertheless, they remained wary of the changes and their consequences:

> After the Ukraine's independence was gained, the Soviet textbooks were abolished, yet there were no new textbooks and there was no real programme of sorts. Then there appeared textbooks, which were heavily politicised. We are not happy with these textbooks, *as they are not scientific*. As a result of all these things, I decided to write a history of Ukraine textbook myself, so as to provide *an objective account of events*.[193]

> I think that the programme is very hard because much time is allocated to politicised information, and not to the development of a world-view. This is happening because Ukraine is a young country, which needs to create its statehood.[194]

Many teachers repeated the assertion that they had been trained in one state, the Soviet Union, with its own specific ideological aims and tasks. However, with the collapse of the USSR and Ukraine's gaining of independence, suddenly they have been called upon to teach the same historical events, yet with differing interpretations, some of which they deem nationalist in content and find difficult to teach:

> Now the narrative is different from the Soviet one, although very little time has passed so as to give a totally objective evaluation of all events. A lot of documents are still not accessible. Although I lived in the Soviet times, and saw myself how these events in reality took place. And now these events are narrated so as to be advantageous to certain politicians and this is wrong.[195]

> In the Soviet textbooks, Ukrainian history is portrayed in the context of Russian history. In the Ukrainian textbooks, there are efforts make one's own history. Up to 1998, there were replacements and juggling, shuffling so as to create this task. New textbooks were introduced with a new nationalistic ideology. And often there are incorrect interpretations of historical facts. Our task is not to 'judge' history but to take

---

193   Lubov', school history teacher, Kharkiv, 4 April 2003.
194   Taisiya, school history teacher, Kharkiv, 4 April 2003.
195   Tatyana, school history teacher, Kharkiv, 23 March 2003.

on facts. Now this is a real problem, like in the Soviet times, there were attempts to judge history.[196]

Whilst many teachers had difficulties in adapting to the demands of the new historical state narrative in Ukraine, nevertheless there was also a groundswell of opinion that some changes occurring were definitely for the better, with a desire for greater choice and greater respect for the individual. Although the state still had a strong control over the historical narrative taught across Ukraine, individuals noted how more choice and opportunity for personal initiative was being slowly introduced into the Ukrainian education system. Indeed, as the following passage demonstrates, there was a growing understanding on the part of the teachers of their 'active' role in the reform process and how they themselves could, in some important respects, dictate change:

> The changes in the education system must be looked on as a state-led process and as an objective process, an everyday proces. At the state-level, the reforms were directed at the widening of creativity of the teacher. Now the teacher has more free-dom and so the pupils can have more creativity also. Actually the reforms *occur more from below* and the Ministry generalises the positive moments, which take place, and tries to pull them out onto the state-level. I consider that this isn't such a bad thing. From the other side, there are not enough prognoses and coordinated re-forms. But our state is young, and the process continues.[197]

In the three study areas, all teachers were in full agreement of the need for children to make up their minds concerning particular historical events and personalities.

The opinions of teachers and university lecturers about the narratives regarding key historical events in Ukraine's history are discussed below in chronological order: the period of Kiev Rus'; the Cossack period with particu-lar attention given towards the two Ukrainian leaders, Bohdan Khmelnytsk'yi and Ivan Mazepa; and Ukraine's time as part of the Soviet Union with attention focusing on the Great Famine of 1932/3 and World War Two.

---

196   Natal'ya, school history teacher, Luhans'k, 5 March 2003.
197   Grigoriy, school history teacher, Luhans'k, 5 March 2003.

Finally, teachers provide some opinions concerning to what extent Russia is depicted as the 'other'.

4.2.1 Kiev Rus'

Soviet historiography defined this period as the beginnings of the Russian state, seeing Kiev as the 'mother of Russian cities'. However, there have been efforts in the Ukrainian history textbooks to introduce an interpretation, which focuses on the importance of the period for the origins of the Ukrainian nation. This approach follows the work of Hrushevskyi, which seeks to legitimise Kiev Rus' as a proto-Ukrainian state.

There was a consensus among teachers in the three study areas concerning the need to tread carefully, feeling that such an interpretation was potentially divisive. Teachers expressed the view that children in Ukrainian schools should learn that from Kiev Rus', the roots of all three of the eastern Slavic peoples, the Russians, Ukrainians and Belarussians, can be drawn:

> Kiev Rus' is taught in the 'History of Ukraine' course. In Russian schools, it is taught in the course, 'History of the Russian people'. Although any understanding at that time of what constitutes the 'Russian nation' or the 'Ukrainian nation' did not exist. If we are to divide the history of Kiev Rus' into the history of Russia or Ukraine, then only arguments emerge and we will not make any concrete decisions.[198]

Some teachers went further, openly criticising the new narrative, as a means to try and delegitimate the relationship between Russia and Ukraine over the centuries:

> The new approach to the origins of Kiev Rus'. Many historians think that the history of Kiev Rus', its traditions after its collapse were transferred to the Galician-Volhynian Kingdom. And Moscow herself later developed on her own. That is to say the opinion of Hrushevskyi is renewing itself. With this they are trying to split the ties between Russia and Ukraine. Yet, all is inter-connected. You have to approach this carefully and not overdo things.[199]

---

198   Irina, school history teacher, Luhans'k, 25 April 2003.
199   Anatoliy, reader in pedagogy, Kharkiv, 22 March 2003.

Overall, many teachers in the interviews were highly aware of the importance of this period within Ukraine's historical development and their feelings on the issue ranged from caution to open anxiety about how the revised historical interpretation attempted to cut ties and links with Russia and portray her as an inalienable 'other'.

4.2.2 The Cossack period

Amongst the teachers there was overall agreement with the narratives in the history textbooks concerning the depiction of Bohdan Khmelnytsk'yi and Ivan Mazepa. Teachers stated that whilst such figures were controversial in Ukrainian society, the role of the teacher was to provide the schoolchildren with an overview of different interpretations:

> Give the child a chance to make his own choice and give a quality appraisal of oc-
> curring events. For example, the position of Bohdan Khmelnytsk'yi in the years of
> battle against Poland. Today there exist a number of different opinions of historians,
> who differently evaluate the role of Bohdan Khmelnytsk'yi in these events. In Po-
> land, there is an opinion, which is totally different from the Ukrainian opinion. In
> Ukraine, there is an opinion which states that signing the treaty with Muscovy was a
> betrayal of his people, and also an opinion that Borden Khmelnytsk'yi, finding him-
> self in this situation took the correct decision, because he kept the state which had
> been created. My task as a teacher is to give the child the Polish point of view, and
> the Ukrainian different points of view so the child made his own choice.[200]

As regards Ivan Mazepa, the situation was very similar. Indeed, one teacher trainer at the Centre for Continuing Education for Kharkiv oblast, spoke about some trial lessons which had taken place in schools across the oblast:

> This figure is ambiguous in Ukraine's history, is he a hero or a traitor? For several
> hundred years he was considered a traitor, and straightaway to now call him a hero
> is not convincing. When I worked in a school, we worked on this issue. The lesson
> ended with the children stating that it is impossible to make any definite conclu-
> sions. One lesson was not enough and the children requested another lesson be
> spent on this subject. These are the lessons of history, which don't end with the

---

sound of the class bell, but instead force the individual to think about the issues at hand. This is the development of a sense of national consciousness.[201]

In these lessons, schoolchildren were given a special project with the aim of evaluating the personality of Ivan Mazepa. The results were found to be very encouraging, with children learning how to analyse different sources and thus make their own personal opinions.

4.2.3 Holodomor: The Great Famine of 1932/3
Turning to the depiction of historical events in Ukraine in the twentieth century, teachers stated that this period, taught in the final two school years, Grades 10 and 11, was the most difficult to teach. This was the case for understandable reasons. Firstly, the teachers felt that this was the period in Ukraine's history where the state textbooks utilised a very 'negative' historical narrative. Teachers, the vast majority of whom had been educated in the Soviet Union and then taught history in Soviet schools, often found this difficult to teach, stating that although mistakes were made during the Soviet times, not everything can be painted in a simplistic 'black and white' fashion, with the Soviet Union and Russia in particular receiving the blame. Secondly, teachers stated that this period of history was difficult to teach because it was still contested in society at large, with the memory of events throughout the twentieth century still fresh in many people's minds. Many stated the difficulties of teaching certain historical narratives, which were often questioned by children, who gained alternative perspectives of such events from outside sources, in particular real witnesses of history, in the form of their parents and grandparents.

The *Holodomor* (Great Famine) of 1932/3 was found to be a particular case in hand. Many teachers expressed the view that previously when they had taught during the Soviet period, coverage of this event in the Soviet history textbooks was sparse if it existed at all, with the tragedy being overlooked for political and ideological reasons. Thus, on the one hand, they saw the lengthy coverage of the event in the new Ukrainian history textbooks being a step in the right direction, with the population gaining an opportunity

---

201 Oksana, methodologist at the Centre for uninterrupted education, Kharkiv Oblast, 6 April 2003.

to learn about a tragic event in their country's history. On the other hand, several teachers expressed a deep unease at the use of this event by the Ukrainian authorities for political purposes.

Whilst they were in agreement that the famine was a prime example of the cruelty of the Stalinist regime, they felt that there was no need for a more 'nationalist' slant to be added. As the director of a school in Luhans'k strongly argued:

> Today, there are lots of problems concerning the Great famine. There is an opinion that the famine was caused by the Russians. But the famine was ideological. In the textbooks is written that *Moskali* (Russians) ruined the Ukrainian people. But here together with Ukrainians were ruined Russians themselves, millions of people perished. The ideology formed this situation. Somebody earned some money from this. You know, bread was sold to Europe. Europe bought this bread. It is possible to make a question, why did Europe, knowing we had a famine, buy this bread? And we say that it was the Russians. I am also a *Moskal*, a Russian, a Don Cossack, therefore should I be kicked every year because the famine took place?[202]

Many other teachers felt that this period needed to be remembered and the reasons for it understood by Ukrainian schoolchildren, but not at the expense of intolerance towards other national groups. From this passage, one can also examine the issue of nationality or ethnicity and how this relates to views held towards the Ukrainian state's nation-building process. Certainly in this case, there is a clear depiction of an ethnic Russian, who was born and lived all his life in Luhans'k, feeling that the Ukrainian state is shifting towards a more 'ethnic' rather than 'civic' understanding of the history of Ukraine, in which the 'Ukrainian people' are given precedence over the 'people of Ukraine'. In this passage, the individual is clearly showing how he feels, that on the basis of his ethnicity, he is being 'disenfranchised' or alienated from the education reform process, occurring in Ukraine.

---

202   Anatoliy, School Director, Luhans'k, 19 February 2003.

4.2.4 World War Two/Great Patriotic War?

This period was found to be the most emotionally charged, with teachers holding highly divisive viewpoints. Teachers repeatedly stated how the interpretation of this period was constantly 'under review' with the historical narrative found in the history textbooks changing throughout the 1990s, making their task even greater. Interestingly, many teachers stated their personal dislike of recent Ukrainian attempts to describe this period as Ukraine's participation in the World War Two, thus rejecting the Soviet understanding of the War as the 'Great Patriotic War':

> In the textbooks, the interpretation is the Soviet Union and fascist Germany are placed together, as both fighting against humanity. In my opinion, this is not a correct interpretation of the evidence. This shouldn't happen. The **Great Patriotic War** for Ukraine, Russia and Belarus, irrespective of changes in the textbooks, remains as the Great Patriotic war.[203]

Moreover, many teachers found that such changes not only went against the wishes of the vast majority of Ukraine's population, but also were highly contradictory to different messages transmitted by the Ukrainian state. In particular, one respondent noted how in the school curriculum there were ongoing attempts to move away from the Soviet conception of this period as the 'Great Patriotic War', while at the same time, 9 May remained a state holiday across Ukraine. This is Victory Day, when the population is encouraged to celebrate the victory of the Soviet Union. Interestingly, however, teachers spoke of a slow shift back towards a Soviet understanding of the war being both 'great' and 'patriotic': shifts which were confirmed in the analysis of recent textbooks discussed in the previous chapter.

Whilst this issue proved controversial, the interpretation of the role of the OUN/UPA in western Ukraine, during the war years sparked passionate debate. During the Soviet years, this movement and their leader, Stepan Bandera, were depicted in the most negative of terms, being classed as 'traitors' and 'bandits.' In contrast, the new Ukrainian historical narrative has tried to provide a more objective interpretation of events, highlighting for example the noble aims of the OUN/UPA in trying to gain Ukraine's inde-

---

203   Galina, school history teacher, Luhans'k, 6 March 2003.

pendence. Many of the teachers interviewed, especially those from Luhans'k and Kharkiv, were deeply critical of this new historical narrative. Again, individuals repeatedly highlighted the need for a more objective appraisal of such contested political events and understood the needs for the Ukrainian state to create a 'united' view concerning events during the war across the whole of Ukraine. However, many felt that the reappraisals had been greatly 'overdone', seeing the new interpretations as attempts to 'rehabilitate' the OUN/UPA so that they are seen as national 'heroes' across Ukraine, just like the veterans of the 'Great Patriotic War'. As one Kharkiv teacher notes:

> This is a painful question in our society. The majority of veterans of the War defended the interests of the country as a part of the USSR. Today, many are still living. Any new appraisal of OUN/UPA creates a sharp and negative reaction from people, who were brought up with Soviet consciousness. But this movement existed and we have to give it an objective appraisal. But it is a different matter; when in the new textbooks and publications OUN/UPA is given three pages and the Soviet underground movement only half a page. This is unfair. We need to look attentively at these things. OUN/UPA without doubt had their own aim and right for existence. They had a good task, the creation of an independent Ukrainian state, but the methods which they used were inappropriate. And the mechanism of the realisation of this idea was not fulfilled. Imagine Hitler allowing the formation of an independent Ukrainian state! This couldn't have happened. Maybe I am going against the 'official' opinion in Ukraine but I do not agree with the conclusions about the role of OUN/UPA after the battle with the German fascist occupiers.[204]

The 'anger' shown by many respondents towards the new narrative clearly demonstrates the grave difficulties the state faces in trying to unite rather than divide the population on this highly emotive issue and the 're-gional' nature of this problem. As one teacher in Luhans'k stated:

> When it became clear what the outcome of the Great Patriotic War would be, the Banderites could not do anything. Western Ukraine, Halychyna, Zakarpattya' and Bukovyna came under Soviet control. And then, they began to fight with teachers, nurses, medical teams, specialists, and Party workers. The Banderites fought with peaceful people, not with the KGB. For example, Lugansk Regional Party Committee sent to L'viv nine times a group of people, who were all then murdered in L'viv

---

204   Anatoliy, reader in pedagogy, Kharkiv, 22 March 2003.

region. These people were instructors, Party workers. Yes, they brought the Party's order words and orders, but their aim was to help the peaceful construction. Young men and women were killed, and it is impossible to justify this. Not everyone agrees with this, but this is how such events occurred. I think that in the coming years, the participants of OUN and UPA will not manage to be rehabilitated. The people will not forgive. This is still a living and actual theme. History should never be rewritten and re-evaluated. *It needs to be evaluated, like it is and only in this way.*[205]

The final sentence of the above passage highlights the insistence on the part of many teachers interviewed that there is only one 'true' history, and thus the new, revised version is simply untrue and thus merits at least contestation if not open rejection. Teachers in the eastern borderlands of Ukraine certainly seemed to 'perceive' these changes as a direct outcome of western Ukrainians gaining political power in Kiev and using it to expand 'their' own historical interpretations onto the rest of Ukraine, at the expense of their 'own' historical viewpoint. This idea is well documented in the following quotation by a school director in Luhans'k:

We are going towards an absurd situation at present. It is known in only one way in the memory of the Soviet people, (and if you like it or not, we are Soviet people, because we grew up in the Soviet Union), Russians, Belarussians and Ukrainians, that the Banderites shot in the back their own people. And today we are making a patriot out of Bandera. And we try to equate them as forces of the freedom of the whole of Europe. *Today, eastern Ukraine does not understand this. Eastern Ukraine considers this to be a big mistake.* I am not saying that we should punish Banderites, it was in the past. Today, it is necessary to unite the Ukrainian people, forget everything which was fifty or sixty years ago, but history must be kept in its place and not be meddled with. If we will change history, then what sort of people are we going to bring up? Lies do not educate a citizen.[206]

Such viewpoints provide evidence of the existence of opposing regional understandings of historical events in Ukraine. An interesting point to consider at this juncture is the importance of 'perception'. The success or failure of state attempts to engineer identity change depends as much on the perception of state policies as on their actual contents. As the statements

---

205   Galina, school history teacher, 6 March 2003.
206   Anatoliy, School Director, Luhans'k, 19 February 2003.

above illustrate, in Ukraine's eastern borderlands there is a definite feeling amongst teachers that the history, which they are now being forced to teach is not only 'untrue' but also unbalanced. In such a fashion, one witnesses a clear demonstration of the spatial dimension of identity politics in Ukraine and of how the 'regional' factor is playing a significant role in Ukraine's education reforms. For several teachers here 'Eastern Ukraine' is viewed as a 'regional construct' whose ideas and views on Ukraine's past are simply not being taken into account as a result of 'western Ukrainian nationalists' gaining power in the government ministries in Kiev. Whilst such results are not representative, nevertheless they provide a highly illuminating picture of how identity change is actually being negotiated in Ukraine.

4.3   Russia as the 'other'

The final section examines how the interviewees in general assess the depiction of Russia within the new Ukrainian historical narrative. A key part of the Ukrainian state's attempts to refashion identities is not only to create an understanding of what it means to be a citizen of Ukraine, but also an understanding of 'who they are not'. National identity is seen through a prism of negation. It is dynamic, defined by the rejection and exclusion of groups deemed not to belong. Triandafyllion underscores the need for scholars to examine more closely the role of the 'other' in national identification and argues that the history of all nations is marked by the presence of 'significant others' who have influenced the development of the identity of the 'in-group'.[207]

In Chapter 3, it was found that indeed the Ukrainian state had endeavoured to portray Russia as Ukraine's inalienable 'other' throughout the school history textbooks. Regarding this issue, interviewees often spoke of their worries. Many stated how the role of education was to create tolerant and civil citizens. However, many interviewees expressed their anxiety that the

---

207   Triandafyllion, A., "National Identity and the 'other' ", *Ethnic and Racial Studies*, 21, 4, July 1998.

depiction of Russia in a negative sense often led to children taking on more 'nationalistic' views towards Russia and Russians:

> When I start to teach the children I straightaway tell myself that I am not guilty for the fact that we have different motherlands. I have the Soviet Union and they have Ukraine. How we understand the world is different. But because we live in one country, we have to find a common language. I think that it is not correct to put information in textbooks that all that happened which was bad came from Moscow. In the textbooks, it is portrayed that Moscow decided everything and Ukraine suffered.[208]

> There are different types of history teacher. Some have a creative approach, some simply teach straight from the textbook. And there are also different textbooks. And some are very aggressive towards Russia. And children who haven't learnt how to analyse facts, begin to take the information on at face value. This is very dangerous, even amongst our pupils; in the essays there are some nationalist undertones. I am afraid that this process will go further.[209]

In particular, individuals often stated that whilst they understood that as a young country, Ukraine needed to create its own historical narrative so as to foster national consciousness, nevertheless the state should be extremely cautious in legitimating the rise of crude nationalism, in which Russia and Russians are stereotyped as the cause of all Ukraine's ills. As a history teacher in Sumy noted:

> Russians come in different guises. The Communist Party oppressed us but the Russian people were not guilty here. If we are to separate from them now, then what does the future hold? Maybe they will help us or we will help them? And we also have our brothers in Belarus'. In Ukraine, there live people of many nationalities. We will educate a sense of national identity, but we should never propagate nationalism. [210]

Similarly many teachers, whilst in full support of a new historical narrative which allows children to learn about the history of their country, simulta-

---

208   Ekaterina, history teacher, Kharkiv, 22 March 2003.
209   Tatyana, school history teacher, Kharkiv, 23 March 2003.
210   Irina, school history teacher, Sumy, 18 April 2003.

neously felt that this history should not be aimed at negating the long history of interaction between the Russian and Ukrainian peoples:

> In the textbooks, there occurs a one-sided tendency. And this is not just in my opinion. If the parents could take a part in the process, then things would be different. But the state decides everything and dictates her tendencies and teachers have to simply fulfil these desires. But teachers in eastern Ukraine see this and try and soften the process. And in western Ukraine, the teachers make a special reference to these tendencies. In western Ukraine the process and the task of the education programme is to show how through history Ukrainians are so poor, so oppressed, so hurt. **Here with us in eastern Ukraine, we don't have this aim.** We are very close to Russia, and we naturally absorbed Russian culture...**Eastern Ukraine has its own mentality.** We have a great closeness to Russia and are a border region. And the tendency, which appears in the textbooks, is very difficult taken on board in schools. Now teachers in Luhans'k region choose which textbook to use, according to their position about disputed historical events.[211]

Again such views bear witness to the construction of a regional identity in 'Eastern Ukraine' which *per se* defines itself *vis-à-vis* 'Western Ukraine'. Within this identity option, contrary to the desires of the central state to portray Russia as Ukraine's 'other', instead the teachers themselves are explicitly stating that in fact the real other for 'Eastern Ukraine' is not Russia, but in fact 'Western Ukraine'.

Whilst there is no outright rejection of the new historical message in the eastern borderlands of Ukraine, this does not equate to outright acceptance of the 'offiical' state narrative. In fact, the results from this research leads one to the conclusion that teachers should be seen not simply as 'transmitters' of information, but as playing a much more significant and active role in the politics of identity in the Ukrainian classroom. If such trends were to occur across the whole of Ukraine, then contrary to the desires of the Ukrainian state, regional differences would not disappear, but in fact would be reinforced. Teachers have the ability to subtly shift the focus of the historical narrative so as to suit the political and historical outlook of the region in which

---

211   Olga, former teacher trainer in history at the Institute for uninterrupted education, Luhans'k oblast, 12 March 2003.

they reside.[212] Whilst such conclusions are in themselves not representative, nevertheless, they justify and illustrate the usefulness of using such micro-level qualitative research methods. Simultaneously they provide a 'regional' perspective on how identity change in Ukraine can be gauged, which rejects the notion that the results of wide-scale quantitative research can be simply extrapolated onto the whole of the country. Instead, the results of this research demonstrate the need for further and deeper examinations of these issues across other areas of Ukraine.

4.4   Schoolchildren's reflections on the 'History of Ukraine'

4.4.1 Kiev Rus'

Regarding this period in Ukraine's history, throughout the interviews it was noticeable that this was an issue, which was being constantly negotiated in the classroom. From the data generated, one witnessed two main lines of argument emerging. Some children and students understood Kiev Rus' as a proto-Ukrainian state, thus taking on the line of historical thought promulgated by Hrushevskyi. As one boy in Luhans'k states:

> They say that it was the beginning of Russia, the Russian politicians, and most of the books that were printed in the time of Soviet rule they said that Kiev Rus' was the beginning of Russia but actually it was Kiev Rus' and Kiev is the capital of Ukraine and we are in the territory of Kiev Rus'.[213]

Similarly a schoolboy in Sumy states how the origins of the Ukrainian nation are found within this period and also 'blames' the fall of Kiev Rus', on outside forces:

---

212   Whilst in the 'field', I spent hours 'observing' history lessons in the schools in the study areas. In several instances, in my opinion, teachers followed a clear 'pick and choose' methodology when utilising the history textbook in which a slightly different accent was placed on events than which the textbook's architects may have wished.

213   Schoolboy, Luhans'k, 14 February 2003.

> From the beginning, Kiev Rus' was a prosperous and developing state. Then Russia and Poland began to divide us. But the Ukrainian people are free-willed. There have been many efforts; our destiny has been difficult and we have forever struggled for our independence. Kiev Rus' was the first manifestation of the Ukrainian nation.[214]

Whilst many interviewees held such a view, there was also perhaps a stronger support for the second view held by many of the teachers seeing this period as the birthplace of all three eastern Slavic peoples. As one schoolgirl states, "I cannot say that this state was our Ukraine itself, it was a long time ago, there weren't as yet the Russian and Ukrainian nations, simply Slavic people."[215] Similarly, Artem, a Grade 11 pupil, summed up by concluding, "Kiev Rus' is the motherland of all the Slavic countries, Russia, Belarus and Ukraine."[216] Many respondents were aware of how hotly disputed this issue was yet displayed a desire for it not to become a symbolic tool for those political forces in Ukraine attempting to divide the Ukrainian and Russian peoples.

4.4.2 The Cossack period

In general the respondents were united in their appraisal of the Cossack period of Ukraine's history. The author noted that the schoolchildren were proud of this period. Concerning the role of Bohdan Khmelnytsk'yi, the responses were united in rejecting the view held in 'nationalist' circles that he was a traitor for entering into a union with Russia. Instead, the respondents were in full agreement with the narrative found in the new historical textbooks stating that Khmelnytsk'yi was forced into joining with Russia at Pereiaslav in 1654, as he had no other alternatives available at that time:

> Bohdan Khmelnytsk'yi was in a very difficult situation because he had two enemies, Russia and Poland, which were very important. Bohdan Khmelnytsk'yi did not conquer all of Poland and Russia was becoming stronger and stronger. He chose to

---

214   Schoolboy, Sumy, 19 March 2003.
215   Schoolgirl, Kharkiv, 23 March 2003.
216   Artem, schoolboy, Kharkiv, 19 March 2003.

unite with Russia, it wasn't really a correct idea, but at that time he had no choice.[217]

Respondents saw Russia as the real culprit 'cheating' Ukraine into joining a union under conditions which Russia was never going to abide by. All were in agreement that Khmelnytsk'yi holds an important part in Ukraine's history and should be regarded as a truly national hero. As one schoolgirl states, "I want to talk about Bohdan Khmelnytsk'yi, he was a great Hetman. Maybe he was the first leader of the Ukrainian people, he was a real leader, and he formed his own state and nation."[218]

Concerning the political figure of Ivan Mazepa, here there was a more contested set of views, with many schoolchildren being aware of how the interpretation of him in today's Ukrainian textbooks differs greatly from the interpretation of him provided in Soviet history textbooks. As one boy in Sumy remarks regarding Mazepa, "He is a hero of the Ukrainian people, because he tried to create an independent Ukraine. But from the point of view of Soviet historiography, he was a traitor as he betrayed the Russian Tsar."[219] The majority of interviews regarded Mazepa as a Ukrainian hero, for not only trying to make Ukraine independent by infamously siding with the Swedish king against the Russians at the battle of Poltava in 1709, but for greatly investing in the country's future, in particular improving education across the country. As one schoolboy states, "When Mazepa came to power, Russia greatly put pressure on Ukrainian culture, Mazepa began to defend it. I consider that Mazepa greatly helped Ukraine in her history and culture."[220] At the same time, Mazepa was also seen in a negative light. As a Grade 11 schoolgirl in Sumy makes clear, "Mazepa wasn't a hero, maybe he did something good, but he wasn't an honest man. In the war with Peter the First, he changed sides and helped the Swedish king."[221] Such views represented a continuation of legitimacy in society for the previous Soviet historical understanding of Mazepa as a 'traitor'.

---

217   Schoolgirl, Luhans'k, 14 March 2003.
218   Schoolgirl, 14 March 2003.
219   Schoolboy, Sumy, 18 March 2003.
220   Schoolboy, Kharkiv, 4 April 2003.
221   Schoolgirl, Sumy, 2003, 18 April 2003.

4.4.3 Holodomor: The Great Famine of 1932/3

Regarding this event, there emerged two schools of thought. Firstly, there was an opinion, which saw the Famine of 1932/3 as a direct conse-quence of actions by the Russian government in Moscow, so as to destroy the Ukrainian nation. The following two quotations demonstrate this:

> It was genocide against the Ukrainian people. Yes, the harvest was not very good, yet there was still a harvest. The grain was collected and transported to Russia. An awful lot of grain was left to rot. Then the repressions began, against cultural fig-ures. They were sent to Siberia or were shot.[222]

> It was against Ukraine. Stalin wanted to conquer Ukraine because of our land, our soil and mineral wealth. Just as Germans wanted to kill Jews, so Russians needed Ukrainians. Russia needed our territory, our people, our nature and that is why they made such a horrible thing as a famine.[223]

Such strongly felt views with the understanding that this was an event of *Russians versus Ukrainians,* was the outcome which many of the teachers had feared may occur. Whilst such individuals were highly vocal and pas-sionate in expressing such viewpoints, there were also voices equally anxious to express a second, different view on events:

> I want to appease the Russian people. The Russian people also greatly suffered at the hands of this state order. The problem was not that either a Russian was bad or a Ukrainian. Everyone suffered. The problem was in the state apparatus.[224]

On the one hand, it is certainly a positive contribution of the new Ukrainian textbooks that children can learn about this tragedy, which previ-ously was washed over by Soviet historiography. However, there is a danger, expressed by many teachers that the Ukrainian state's search for a historical narrative to legitimate the current state itself, means that at certain junctures, such as this one, the narrative is highly negative towards the influence of other nations, in the most part, Russians, on Ukraine's development.

---

222   Schoolgirl, Kharkiv, 4 April 2003.
223   Schoolgirl, Luhans'k, 15 March 2003.
224   Schoolboy, Kharkiv, 4 April 2003.

4.4.4 World War Two/Great Patriotic War?

Whilst many teachers expressed their view that the term, the 'Great Patriotic War' as used in the Soviet times should not be discarded, amongst the younger generation, opinions were more divided, with opinions split between two opposing viewpoints:

> For us, Ukrainians and Russians, this was the Great Patriotic War. I know that at present there is a movement in Ukrainian society, which thinks that for Ukraine it was WWII from 1941 to 1943, when   the Germans left the territory of Ukraine. I think that this is wrong. *Our Ukrainians* fought in Ukraine,   in the Caucasus, and in Russia, and then fought all the way across Europe to Berlin, in which fought Ukrainians, Russians, Armenians, all nationalities.[225]

Whilst this opinion was in agreement with the teachers for the continued use of the term, 'Great Patriotic War', the opposing opinion, was highly critical of Russia; "Russia betrayed Ukraine in this war. Ukraine could have fought for herself if her people had not suffered during the Famine and the repressions. There weren't any supplies of arms to Ukraine, nor military forces."[226]

Such differences concerning the war were reflected in the next theme under consideration, namely the role of OUN/UPA in western Ukraine during the war years. Here, three main viewpoints emerged. Firstly, the opinion was expressed that it was very difficult to 'judge' the actions of the OUN/UPA. On the one hand their goal of the creation of a Ukrainian state was noble. However their means of achieving this were less admirable. As one school-boy remarks:

> Concerning OUN/UPA, I don't have a definite point of view. They sort of struggled for independence, a good deed. Yet on the other side, they fought against their own people, burnt villages, killed people and took the food. It is difficult to say if they are heroes or not.[227]

---

225   Schoolgirl, Kharkiv, 3 April 2003.
226   Schoolgirl, Kharkiv, 3 April 2003.
227   Schoolboy, Kharkiv, 4 April 2003.

Alongside this neutral evaluation of events, the remaining two view-points are far less neutral. The first is highly supportive of the role of OUN/UPA seeing them as 'freedom fighters' and this period as yet more evidence of the never ceasing desire of the Ukrainian people to build their own independent state. As one schoolgirl in Kharkiv notes:

> To look onto history as a whole, then Ukraine has overcome all difficulties. There was always a national independence movement. Even when we were part of *Soviet Russia*, during the Second World War, OUN/UPA tried to create an independent Ukraine, although it turned out not to be possible.[228]

This viewpoint also highlights a theme, which occurred occasionally throughout the interviews with schoolchildren of mixing up the 'Soviet Union' with 'Soviet Russia'. Such a mistake is highly significant in demonstrating the effects of the new historical narrative's negative evaluation of the Soviet period, in which, as illustrated in Chapter 3, the Soviet Union is described as a *pseudo*-Russian state and Ukraine as her oppressed, internal colony.

The final and third viewpoint expressed the old Soviet understanding of OUN/UPA and its leader, Bandera, as enemies of the people and 'traitors', in vivid terms:

> Western Ukraine in the period of World War II made an attempt to break away from the USSR, but it failed. Banderites joined with the Germans who helped them to kill their own people, Ukrainians, who the Banderites pointed out to be killed. Bande-rites tried to make a new country on the corpses of their fellow-countrymen.[229]

Here the regional nature of historical consciousness in Ukraine is clearly portrayed, corresponding to the teachers' evaluation of this period. Efforts to justify the actions of OUN/UPA are seen by many schoolchildren as unjustified, and being pushed forward by a 'western Ukrainian' lobby who desire their rehabilitation. As one schoolboy openly states, "Now in the government there is a group of people from western Ukraine, they look to the west and not to the east."[230] Also of real significance, the regional under-

---

228   Schoolgirl, Kharkiv, 4 April 2003.
229   Schoolgirl, Luhans'k, 5 March, 2003.
230   Schoolboy, Kharkiv, 4 April 2003.

standing of spatial politics in Ukraine seemingly is being passed on here from generation to generation, with children just like their teachers seeing the real 'other' for them to be 'western Ukraine' and not in fact Russia.

In general, schoolchildren expressed a desire to learn about the history of their country and many stated how they enjoyed it and realised that they were now able to learn about events and political figures, which were previously 'blank spots' in the Soviet historiography. However, several individuals also stated the difficulties and pressures they themselves faced as children learning history in a period of such large changes within their country, stating how, as well as gaining a historical perspective from the textbooks, they often gained also an alternative perspective from their parents and grandparents at home, thus being forced to decide which narrative to support:

> That is the most difficult thing about the present day history books is that earlier about fifteen years ago, our parents were taught about different things from what we learn now and we have to make a big decision. Whether it is this way or that way, or maybe somewhere in the middle.[231]

Furthermore, individuals also expressed disillusionment with the new Ukrainian historical narrative, drawing specific attention to the fact that no real changes have occurred in terms of methodology, with the state, either Soviet or now Ukrainian, simply using history specifically for its own political ends. As one schoolboy in Luhans'k succinctly sums up:

> I have read the Soviet and new Ukrainian textbooks. Soviet textbooks state that The Party is the brightest and best. Bourgeoisie and capitalism are bad. In the dictionary the word 'patriotism' was explained as a love for one's motherland. But in bourgeois capitalist society it does not exist. People are bad and they do not understand patriotism. In the modern Ukrainian textbooks, it is stated that the Party, this is bad. It killed many people and under her rule, nothing good at all happened. It is not clear who to believe, it is very difficult. The society has become democratic, but we do not have real freedom of speech. What the authors were told to write, they then wrote.[232]

---

231 Schoolboy, Luhans'k, 14 February 2003.
232 Schoolboy, Luhans'k, 5 March 2003.

Such statements demonstrate that the schoolchildren are far from mere passive recipients of a state narrative fed to them from above. Instead, they are actively negotiating the historical narrative, receiving information from various sources, including their school textbook, their schoolteacher as well as their family and friends. Even more revealing are remarks of schoolboys in Kharkiv, one stated, "In many textbooks, Russia is portrayed as a hostile enemy of us. And even if I don't agree with the narrative of the textbook, in an exam, I am forced to write down the narrative from the textbook. If I don't, I will gain low marks."[233] After this comment in this particular interview, when the author asked the remaining children about this viewpoint, the vast majority were in full agreement. This particular occasion serves as an illustration of a wider held feeling amongst the vast majority of the schoolchildren, who participated in the group interviews in Luhans'k, Kharkiv and Sumy, which is summed up by the following remark by another boy in Kharkiv. "In our universities, there are Arabs, Indians, Chinese, Americans and nobody has a go at them. So why do we have to hate our near neighbours, with whom we have interacted for years and centuries?"[234] Whilst many children were prepared to accept some of the Ukrainian state narrative's representations of the Russian *state* as being hostile towards Ukraine over the centuries, nevertheless they saw no need on account of previous perceived historical injustices to hold an open dislike of Russians as a *people*.

---

233   Schoolboy, Kharkiv, 4 April 2003.
234   Schoolboy, Kharkiv, 4 April 2003.

4.5   Conclusions

The assumption that history education in Ukraine is progressing very well on account of the fact that the same textbooks are used across the whole of Ukraine and there has been a lack of outward protest to the changes is rejected.[235] On the contrary, this chapter has demonstrated that in Ukraine's eastern borderlands, teachers and children alike are highly active in negotiating the new historical narrative. Whilst the new Ukrainian historical narrative up to the twentieth century is generally accepted, the depiction of events such as the Famine of 1932/33 and the role of OUN/UPA in the war years come under great scrutiny, as does the overall negative representation of Russia's influence on Ukraine's history. It was found that the role of teachers was not always simply to 'transfer' the state's desired historical message. They themselves often held opinions concerning debated historical events, which were contrary to the 'official' version of events.

This research not only demonstrates that the 'official' historical narrative is being contested, but perhaps more importantly, highlights the *mechanisms and processes* through which such negotiation and contestation takes place. In the case of the teachers who disagree with certain historical interpretations, they have not chosen to reject openly this historical message, but rather to appropriate selectively certain 'messages'. This phenomenon could be called **'inclusion without exclusion'** in which individuals *subtly change the accent or focus* away from a 'nationalist' or 'negative' stance towards Russia to a more tolerant stance, which aims to promote rather than negate Ukraine's historical interactions with Russia. In doing so, they simultaneously reinforce a particular 'regional' understanding of past events.

In this fashion, rather than the state message 'from above' replacing regional identities, in fact a contestation is taking place. Certain parts of the state's message are received and taken on board, certain messages are outwardly rejected and many messages are being simultaneously adapted so as to fit in with the existing regional understandings of Ukraine's past. Teachers felt that the content of the historical narrative was becoming too

---

235   Popson, N, "Conclusion: Regionalism and Nation Building in a Divided Society", in Kuzio, T., and D'Anieri, P., (ed.), *Dilemmas of State-Led Nation Building in Ukraine*, Westport, CT: Praeger, 2002: 201.

'nationalistic' owing to influence from western Ukrainians who are now controlling certain ministries in Kiev. In this respect, the term 'Eastern Ukraine', which was used on numerous occasions throughout the interviews, can be seen here as a constructed regional identity, which acts to 'protect their views'. Rather than viewing Russia as the 'other' it instead sees 'Western Ukraine' as the 'other' in terms of culture, language and historical memory.

Turning to the younger generations, whilst certain individuals have 'received' the state narrative and accepted it at face value, others were highly critical of it, seeing it as a crude attempt to (re)construct identities in Ukraine, using a highly negative representation of Russia as a cruel 'other.' In such a fashion, many children were making two interconnected arguments. One, they were happy to learn about the history of Ukraine and understand what it means to be 'Ukrainian' today. Two, they were simultaneously unwilling to fully accept the 'official' narrative, which seeks to negate the role of Russia and Russians throughout Ukraine's history. Here, again, we see a clear 'regional' perspective emerging and one in which their imaginations of what is 'Ukraine' today differ from the 'official' state doctrine. Interestingly, one can witness to some degree generational differences between the teachers and the schoolchildren regarding certain contentious issues, with children engaging issues and events with, understandably, less 'ideological baggage' than their adult counterparts. At the same time, it was also relevant to witness how on many other issues the children held very similar and strongly-held views like their teachers, for example concerning the negation of Russia's role in Ukraine's history and also the role of OUN/UPA in the war years of the 1940s.

In conclusion, children and teachers alike are willing to (re)fashion their own identities, learn about 'their' past, but *actively pick and choose* which interpretations they accept or reject. An understanding of Russia as Ukraine's 'other' is highly contested and often rejected. Such empirical findings, in full measure, demonstrate that 'regional' historical viewpoints are still present in the politics of identity across Ukraine. Regarding some of the most hotly disputed parts of Ukraine's history, teachers and children alike in Ukraine's eastern borderlands have different understandings of *where they are from*, from the 'official' state version. In particular, many individuals are unhappy about the contents of some of the 'official' narratives. In this fashion, the results of this research indeed highlight an implicit desire of people in these areas for 'their' understanding of the past to be heard and also to make explicit their feelings of disenfranchisement from the state-led process of 'nation building' in Ukraine. Children as well as the adult teachers in their schools are highly active in these processes, not simply passive absorbers of information and are constantly (re)evaluating their place in the spatial dimension of identity politics across Ukraine.

From one angle these results demonstrate the task of (re)fashioning identities across Ukraine is one which will take a great deal of time. The task of creating a unifying rather than a divisive 'national history' is proving extremely difficult, yet simultaneously vital. However, while certain events discussed above are still highly contested, it is important not to forget that there are many strands of Ukraine's history which teachers and children alike agree upon.

Finally, the results indicate the importance of taking into account 'perception' towards state policies when judging their relative success. As highlighted in Chapter 3, the evaluation of OUN/UPA in the new historical textbooks does not take such a crude 'nationalising' stance that many teachers and schoolchildren alike spoke about. In many respects, such a reaction demonstrates the fact that the Soviet understanding of 'nationalism' as a dirty word, still remains today in Ukraine's eastern borderlands. However, such findings are highly relevant for the success or failure of the Ukrainian state's efforts to instigate identity change. For example, if a small minority perceives a state policy as 'nationalising' and this minority is spread across the whole country, then its influence on events will be negligible. However, if such a view is held in a concentrated area by a large mass of people, then the state faces a much greater danger. The results outlined in this chapter certainly demonstrate that the population of Ukraine's eastern borderlands is highly critical of the 'official' depiction of certain events in Ukraine's past, in particular events during the war years of the early 1940s. Whilst no major protests have emerged, the Ukrainian state nevertheless needs to be aware that the historical narrative aims to promote 'uniting' rather than 'dividing' Ukraine's population.

5 'Who we are?' and 'Who we are not?' Understanding the Importance of the 'Region'

This chapter examines perceptions and understandings of the 'regional' factor in Ukraine's identity politics. Commencing with an assessment of regional historical narratives using 'regional' geography and history textbooks, the author explores the extent they complement or contradict the state's 'official' narrative. In this way, the author can gauge to what extent the view of education elites in the regions actually corresponds to the 'official' view of Ukraine's history, laid out by the centre in Kiev. In addition, data generated from the in-depth interviews, introduced in the previous chapter is analysed further to examine how individuals reflect on the importance of the 'region' in Ukraine today. Finally, the chapter concludes with an evaluation of individuals' reflections on Russia.

5.1 Regional narratives: complementing or contradicting the state narrative?

Since 1991 schoolchildren have begun not only to learn about the 'History of Ukraine', but also to learn about their native region in a subject called *Heohrafiya ridnoho krayu* (Geography of the native region).

5.1.1 Luhans'k

In Luhans'k, the author discovered that the local education officials had introduced another subject entitled *Istoriya i kul'tura ridnoho krayu. Luhans'ka oblast* (History and culture of the native region: Luhans'k region).[236] The two

---

236 *Prohrama spetskursi z istorii ta kul'turi ridnoho krayu Luhans'koi oblasti (z naidavnishix chasiv do poch. XXst.) dlya uchniv 8-9 klasiv*, Luhans'k, 2002. This document was given to the author by a history teacher at one of the schools, in which interviewing took place.

textbooks below were analysed, both of which were published in the Ukrainian language.

* Pankrat'ev, O.A., *Heohrafiya ridnoho krayu: Luhans'ka oblast, 5 klas,* Luhans'k: Yantar, 2001. (Geography of the native region: Luhans'k region, Grade 5).
* Horelik, A.F., Virova, T,V., Krasil'nikiv, K.R., *Istoriya ridnoho krayu (Luhans'ka Oblast'),* Ch.1, Luhans'k: Luhan', 1995. (History of the native region: Luhans'k region, part 1).

Commencing with the textbook used in Grade 5, particular attention is given to the settlement of the region jointly by Russians and Ukrainians. In doing so, the narrative veers away from the Ukrainian national-statist narrative which excludes the possibility of Russians settling this region, seeing them rather as the products of Tsarist and Soviet immigration policies. In contrast, the text argues that Russians are indigenous settlers, especially in the southeastern parts of the oblast when it states:

> The western part (of the region) was settled by Zaporizhzhian Cossacks. The southeast became the land of the *Vyis'ka Donsk'oho*, (the Don Cossacks). Cossacks were brave and experienced fighters and reliably defended their land...for a long time here have lived the descendants of the Zaporizhzhian and Don Cossacks, the Ukrainians and Russians.[237]

Similarly regarding the industrialisation of the region, the influx of people to the newly developing coalmines and factories is not portrayed as 'waves of Russian immigrants', but rather as a natural process. Indeed, the text highlights the 'multinational' nature of the Donbas, when it states:

> In the twentieth century at the time of the Great Patriotic War, the economy of our region was totally ruined. In order to rejuvenate the mines and factories after the war people arrived from all over the huge Soviet Union. Ossetians and Belarussians, Kazaks and Uzbeks shoulder-to-shoulder worked in construction, in the mineshafts and in the steelworks. Many remained here. Our grandfathers and

---

237   Pankrat'ev, O.A., *Heohrafiya ridnoho krayu: Luhans'ka oblast, 5 klas,* Luhans'k: Yantar, 2001: 76.

great-grandfathers together built a multinational house – the Donbas, in which we all now live.[238]

This depiction strongly adheres to the Soviet image of the region as the 'kochegarka', the boiler house of the whole Soviet Union. This regional identity, which arose in Donbas through the Soviet years, had its roots in the ideology of 'Soviet internationalism,' with the importance of national identities substituted by identities strongly linked to work and heavy industry. Similarly, the text concludes that, "our multinational culture was created in the main by two Slavic peoples – the Russians and Ukrainians. Much has come into our culture from the first inhabitants of the 'wild fields' – the Cossacks."[239] In this fashion, the text continues focusing attention on the 'free-living' nature of the Cossacks, seen as founders of the region. Yet, whilst the 'Cossack myth' is utilised, it is not solely to justify Ukrainian national mythologies. Instead, it is used to justify the joint settlement of the region by Russians and Ukrainians and highlight the roots of the region's multinational nature.

Regarding language use, the narrative here is ambiguous. It begins by stating, "Our region is multi-lingual. The inhabitants of our cities traditionally speak the Russian language. The population of most of the villages speak the Ukrainian language." The narrative continues by quoting from the Ukrainian Constitution of the state guaranteeing "the right for the learning of the native language and the instruction of the native language." The text states: "the native language is transferred in families from parents to children. The family itself chooses which language to speak. In multi-national families, several languages are spoken; Russian, Ukrainian, the native language comes from the parents."[240] The narrative, by highlighting the 'natural' nature of the choice of native language, represents perhaps an implicit attack on efforts to 'impose' language use by state authorities. Yet, the narrative continues by drawing attention to another part of the Constitution which states that: "The state language in Ukraine is Ukrainian. A citizen of Ukraine must not have difficulties in using the state language. The Ukrainian language is taught in all of the schools in our region." Nonetheless, the section concludes by using the

---

238   Pankrat'ev, O.A., *Heohrafiya ridnoho krayu*, 76.
239   *Ibid.*, 79.
240   *Ibid.*, 82.

old Soviet-style legitimation of the use of Russian, thinly veiled behind the rhetoric of 'the language of international communication.' As the text states: "The state facilitates the learning of languages of international communication. With the development of international business, in people there arises the demand to possess foreign languages, therefore children learn them and so do adults."[241]

Overall this narrative regarding language use is intriguing. It represents a 'balancing act' in arguing that the continued use and instruction of Russian in the region is legitimated by the Ukrainian Constitution. Yet, at the same time, it is also careful not to veer too far away from the 'official' state rhetoric. Whilst there is not an *open* rejection or protest against linguistic ukrainisation, nevertheless, the process is not especially welcomed. In general, this textbook's depiction of the history of the region rejects the 'official' narrative's desire to represent Russia and Russians as an 'other'. The text outlines a regional historical narrative, concentrating on the joint interaction and settlement of the region by both Russians and Ukrainians. Also the rapid development of the region under Soviet rule is not symbolised as being a period of oppression or colonisation. Instead, the 'multinational' nature of the region developed as a result of 'natural' processes, brought about by Soviet modernisation processes.

The textbook regarding the history of Luhans'k oblast concentrates on the settlement of the region in the sixteenth and seventeenth centuries. The narrative complements that of the Grade 5 geography textbook in presenting the joint role of both Russian and Ukrainian Cossacks in settling the 'wild field'. However, the text goes into further detail. For example, it depicts the historical relations between the Zaporizhzhian and Don Cossacks as symbolising the roots of the friendly co-existence of Russians and Ukrainians in the region. As the text states:

> The history of the relations between the Zaporizhzhian and Don Cossacks in the seventeenth century bears evidence that between them there existed a genuine military brotherhood, a union. Although the relations between them were not always ideal, friendly relations were not broken off. Between these two fellow free people, lay ethnic, religious kinship, the same tasks; guard their lands from Tatar raids and

---

241   *Ibid.*, 82.

defend their independence from the Muscovite (and for the Zaporizhzhians from the Polish) government. The historic importance of our lands in the seventeenth century is concluded in the fact that they were a major bridge, uniting the Zaporizhzhian Sich' and the Don Cossacks.[242]

Furthermore, the narrative analyses the different patterns of settlement of the northern and southern parts of the region. In particular, it focuses on the 'Ukrainian' nature of the northern parts, which were part of the *Sloboz-hanshchyna* region, with its centre in Kharkiv:

> In the history of our region the role of Ukrainian peasants and Cossacks, who ar-
> rived in the Izium and Ostrogozhskiy *slobodi* regions, was enormous. The *Slobodi*
> did not just defend our lands from attacks from Crimean Tatars. Most importantly,
> they laid the foundation for the future peaceful life and created the varied agricul-
> tural production. The *Sloboda* colonisation was agricultural and many settlements
> founded by the *Slobodi* peasants and Cossacks, exist to this day. Although they
> were from the start subordinated to the Moscow government, the Slobodi upheld
> the traditions and culture of the Ukrainian people in this land. [243]

In contrast, the rooted nature of Russian influence in the region, especially in its southeast parts, is explained by the role of the Don Cossacks:

> The Don Cossacks in the eighteenth century played a remarkable influence on the
> path of the history of our region. The colonisation by the prosperous Dons of the
> southeast territories of modern day Luhans'k region, laid the way for their wide agri-
> cultural opening up. Here lies the specific characteristic for the Donbas, a mixed
> population, including Russians and Ukrainians.[244]

In this fashion, the narrative repeats the claims of the Grade 5 textbook,
concerning the rootedness of both the Russian and Ukrainian peoples in the
region.

Overall, these two textbooks provide a distinct, regional perspective
which, concerning key issues, contradicts the narrative found in the all-

---

242   Horelik, A.F., Virova, T.V., Krasil'nikiv, K.R., *Istoriya ridnoho krayu (Luhans'ka Oblast'),* Ch.1, Luhans'k: Luhan', 1995: 122-123.
243   Horelik, A.F., Virova, T.V., Krasil'nikiv, K.R., *Istoriya ridnoho krayu,* 133.
244   *Ibid.,* 133.

Ukrainian historical textbooks. They focus on the co-founding and the peaceful co-existence of Russians and Ukrainians in the region over the centuries and in doing so, severely problematise the desire of the state-led nation-building project to represent Russia as an 'other.' This discourse attempts to legitimate the current mixed Russian-Ukrainian nature of identities in the region, seen as the natural culmination of historical processes. In contrast it rejects the Ukrainian national historical narrative which sees such a situation as 'unnatural', created by the 'de-ukrainisation' of the local population during Tsarist and Soviet times.

5.1.2 Kharkiv

The following textbooks were analysed:

- Sadkina, V, I., *Geografiya rodnogo kraya, 5 klas*, Khar'kov: Skorpion, 2001. (The geography of the native region: Grade 5).
- Shyl'zhenko, L, S, *Geografiya rodnogo kraya: Slobozhanshchyna, 5 klas*, Khar'kov: Ranok, 2001. (The geography of the native region: Slobozhanshchyna, Grade 5).
- Kononenko, O. E., Shul'zhenko, L, S., *Kharkivshchynoznavstvo*, Kharkiv: Gymnaziya, 2002. (Knowledge about the Kharkiv region).

Commencing with Sadkina's textbook, attention is paid to the settlement of the region by both Russians and Ukrainians:

> In order to defend her southern borders, the Muscovite government at the end of the sixteenth and beginning of the seventeenth centuries sent to the 'wild field' servicemen the *streltsov*, (shooters). They and the Ukrainian Cossacks were the founders of the region, the *slobodi*, (this word is derived from the word 'freedom', that is to say the region was settled by free people).[245]

The narrative describes the founding of Kharkiv and the city's development in the eighteenth and nineteenth centuries. Regarding events in the twentieth century, the narrative focuses on Kharkiv's period of being the capital of the UkrSSR from 1919 to 1934. It states:

---

245   Sadkina, V, I., *Geografiya rodnogo kraya, 5 klas*, Khar'kov: Skorpion, 2001: 15.

For Kharkiv it was an incredibly important fact that it was the capital of Ukraine from 1919 to 1934. With this was linked the grandiose construction of industrial enterprises, the opening up of cultural and social life, of science and the enlightenment of our region.[246]

The narrative also focuses on the Great Patriotic War between 1941/1945:

> A tragic imprint on the history of Kharkiv region left behind the "Great Patriotic War" of 1941-45. For Kharkiv, hard and bloody battles were fought and the city several times passed into different hands. From October 1941 until August 1943, the fascists occupied Kharkiv as well as other cities and parts the region. The occupiers set up in the Kharkiv region a regime of bloody terror; 280,000 peaceful citizens were killed; the elderly, women and children. Also thousands of Kharkivites died from hunger and disease. 160,000 people were taken to the forced labour camps in Germany... The liberation day of Kharkiv, the 23 August 1943, has become a joyous celebration of victory for Kharkivites of all generations.[247]

Such an account clearly demonstrates a rejection of Ukrainian national historical narratives, which attempt to discard the Soviet term, 'Great Patriotic War'. Instead, for this region a 'Soviet' narrative of this period holds sway with the German fascists as the only 'other'. Regarding the national composition of the region, the importance of tolerance of other nationalities and civil values is underlined:

> Probably, in your class there are children of different nationalities, and this totally does not hinder you all learning together, participating in games, sport competitions and in general being friends. Your class - this is a small part of the Kharkiv region. And it has representatives of over 100 nationalities. The largest number of course is Ukrainians, 63 people out of every 100. For the most part, they live in rural districts, in Valkovsk, for example, 92 people out of 100 are Ukrainian. But in those districts where there have grown large industrial enterprises, (factories and electric power stations), where the population arrived for construction, from far away, the national composition is mixed. [248]

---

246   *Ibid.*, 18.
247   *Ibid.*, 18-19.
248   *Ibid.*, 85.

Finally the role of Russians in the region is described, their large numbers in the region explained not as the product of Tsarist and Soviet immigration policies, but owing to other factors, in particular to the borderland status of the region throughout its history:

> The Russians take up the second place, by numbers. They constitute a third of the population of the Kharkiv region (Remember the history of the settlement of our region). This is explained not only by historical reasons, but also by the closeness of the state border with Russia.[249]

The Shyl'zenko textbook provides an alternative narrative for children in Grade 5. In particular, as the title suggests, the textbook makes a direct association of the Kharkiv region with the historical region of *Slobozhanshchyna*. Indeed the lack of correlation between the 'historic' and 'administrative' boundaries of regions in Ukraine is implicitly highlighted when the text states:

> As the most important city in Slobozhanshchyna, Khar'kov has the most influence on the nieghbouring oblasts – Sumy, Poltava and also Donetsk and Lugansk – territories of which were previously part of Slobozhanshchyna. In connection to the fact that the 'Sloboda' region does not have any generally recognised borders, when people write the address of a city, they indicate only the name of one of the oblasts, and the name of the country, Ukraine.[250]

Regarding the settlement of the region, the narrative subtly varies from the previous one. Instead of highlighting the joint efforts of Russians and Ukrainians, only the Ukrainian Cossacks are mentioned, symbolised as peaceful and free-living people. As the text states:

> The historic fate of our freedom-loving and able people was heroic. Our ancestors mastered previously uncultivated land, defended it from warring and cruel neighbours and kept for us our native land. From the onset, the free Cossacks were the first to come and settle here from Ukraine to the so-called 'wild field'. Then, the people of Ukraine in our region created a modern civilisation, that is to say, that

---

249   *Ibid.*, 85.
250   Shyl'zhenko, L.S., *Geografiya rodnogo kraya: Slobozhanshchyna, 5 klas*, Khar'kov: Ranok, 2001: 7.

everything which was built, was by the *Ukrainian people* – cities, schools, churches and roads.[251]

Furthermore, the narrative asserts the importance of an attachment to one's native region. As the text states:

> For many of us the understanding of the *rodina* (motherland), is invisibly connected with the house, where you were born and grew up…It is necessary for everyone together to guard and love the motherland – the land, which feeds us, our native region.[252]

Finally, the multinational nature of the region is embraced:

> Together with the Cossacks, Russians, Belarussians, Germans, Poles, Jews, Tatars have settled here…They all put something of their own way of life into the way of life and unrepeatable culture of the Sloboda region, enriched it with their own national celebrations, traditions. In recent times, Azeri, Georgians and Ossetians have also settled here. The majority of them speak Russian, but each also holds their own native language. Learn languages, as each new language – this is new friends…It is necessary to know and to respect the customs and traditions of each people – then each person will be a real friend to you and help in times of misfortune.[253]

Thus, in a similar vein to the previous textbook, children are called upon to respect and tolerate all national groups.

Kononenko's book, 'Knowledge about the Kharkiv region' textbook differs from the previous two in that it is written in the Ukrainian language, and is designed for use in Grades 8 and 9, thus providing a more detailed history of the native region for the older children. The narrative commences, telling the reader of the border status of the region, drawing attention to the lack of any 'natural' or visible border in the region along its state border with Russia. Regarding the key period of its settlement, the joint efforts of both Ukrainians and Russians are denoted:

---

251   *Ibid.*, 3.
252   *Ibid.*, 4.
253   *Ibid.*, 41.

Nearing the seventeenth century, the mutual influence of Ukrainian and Russian cultures became important for the historic fate of the region. The Ukrainians and Russians with joint efforts settled and maintained the territory of *Slobozhanshchyna* in a cruel struggle with raiders. They created a spiritual and cultural life, which arose from the cultural and national trends of both the Ukrainians and the Russians.[254]

Moreover, the text continues by describing how, in the bloody years between 1917-1921, whilst the ultimate victory of the Bolsheviks in the region was aided by forces arriving from Soviet Russia, nonetheless, Bolshevism already had support in the region. In the all-Ukrainian history textbooks, Bolshevism and the onset of Soviet rule is portrayed as a 'foreign force' and an 'other', here the picture is more ambiguous. Similarly, the text describes in great detail the war years 1941-45, a war still remembered as the 'Great Patriotic War':

> The Great Patriotic War has finished. But the population of the Kharkiv region remembers and long will remember the days, when the fate of the city was sealed, it still remembers those, who gave their lives for the future of our people. There is no city, no village, where there have not been immortalised the feats of the heroes of the war.[255]

Finally, the narrative continues the discourse of the other textbooks in focusing on the co-existence and mutual influence which both Russians and Ukrainians have had in the region.

> The phenomenon of *Slobozhanshchyna* is a result of the history of the interaction of Ukrainian and Russian cultures. *Slobozhanshchyna* holds a unique place for the formation of close Ukrainian-Russian relations. The city of Kharkiv has its own place in international affairs as one of the corners of the triangle of international relations between *Ukrainian Kiev, Russian Moscow and Ukrainian-Russian Kharkivshchyna (Kharkiv region).*[256]

---

254   Kononenko, O.E., Shul'zhenko, L.S., *Kharkivshchynoznavstvo*, Kharkiv: Gymna-ziya, 2002: 68.

255   *Ibid.*, 213.

256   *Ibid.*, 226.

This quotation sums up succinctly the fact that Kharkiv defines its regional identity in respect to Russia, seeing itself as a 'special' case owing to
its 'bridging role' between Russia and Ukraine. Overall, these three textbooks
readily highlight the importance given to a regional historical narrative in
Kharkiv. The regional identity which is being espoused, embraces the
Ukrainian character of the region and the importance of Ukrainian Cossacks
in its development. Nevertheless it also gives attention to the role of Russians
in the region's settlement and subsequent development. Thus, it acts as an
alternative to state-led attempts to portray Russia as an unalterable 'other'
and legitimates the desires of regional elites to maintain economic and
cultural links with Russia.

5.1.3 Sumy

Here, only one textbook was analysed:

- Leont'eva, H. H., Tuleneva., V. O., Yatsenko, D. I., Cherepanova, E.
  O., *Heohrafiya ridnoho krayu: 5 klas*, Sumy: Nota bene, 2002, pp.1-
  74. (The geography of the native region: Grade 5).

In contrast to Luhans'k and Kharkiv, education authorities in Sumy saw
no need for any 'additional' textbooks relating to the history of the region, and
instead, chose to follow the state guidelines, providing just one textbook, to
be used only in Grade 5 of the schooling system.

Furthermore, the textbook pays little attention to the previously described key issues such as settlement of the oblast and national composition.
The only point of relevance is how the geographical position of the region is
analysed, with it being part of the historic *Slobozhanshchyna* region. The text
states:

Ukraine is divided into historical-ethnic regions. They are determined by the character of historical development, the geographical position of the territory and the links
with other people. Therefore, the northeastern part of Ukraine is a part of a region
called *Slobozhanshchyna*, from the word 'freedom'. *Slobozhanshchyna* is closely

connected with Russia. Here have interacted Ukrainian and Russian customs, ways of life, and even language.[257]

Whilst the existence of regional historical narratives in Kharkiv and Lu-hans'k may demonstrate a desire on the part of these regional authorities to contest the all-Ukrainian historical narrative, in Sumy, just as intriguingly, the very absence of a coherent regional historical narrative may indicate that local education elites *per se* fully accept the 'official' state narrative. Also, the lack of any explicit contestation of the 'official' state narrative may be linked to the weakness of a specific regional identity in Sumy and the area's political passivity in contrast to Kharkiv and Luhans'k. A further factor here which cannot be excluded is the issue of financial resources. In relation to Luhans'k and Kharkiv, Sumy is very much a 'rural backwater' with fewer financial resources available to utilise on political projects.

The results of this analysis of regional textbooks highlight key differences in how regional elites across Ukraine's eastern borderlands are in the process of negotiating state-led nation-building in the realm of historical education. Across the three study areas, the narratives differ to one another, and sometimes directly contradict key parts of the narrative, found in the all-Ukrainian history textbooks. This is especially the case in Luhans'k and Kharkiv. Here, the interaction and co-existence of Russians and Ukrainians is portrayed in a positive manner, seen as key parts of the 'multinational' cultures of the oblasts, which must be tolerated, respected and celebrated. In Kharkiv, great attention is placed on the historical myth of *Slobozhanshchyna*, and a regional identity involving Russian and Ukrainian interaction. In Luhans'k, attention is placed on the specific Donbas regional identity, which arose in the Soviet times, idealising in truly Soviet internationalist style, the multinational and working class nature of the population.

---

257   Leont'eva, H.H., Tuleneva, V.O., Yatsenko, D.I., Cherepanova, E.O., *Heohrafiya ridnoho krayu: 5 klas*, Sumy: Nota bene, 2002: 4-5.

5.2 The importance of the 'region': reflections from the classroom

From interviews with school directors and teachers, many interviewees were acutely aware of the regional differences across Ukraine, with two main themes emerging. First, several of the teachers expressed the opinion that regional differences play a huge role in domestic politics in Ukraine and the so-called 'east-west' divide was real. Holders of this viewpoint were very keen to stress that eastern Ukrainians should not be 'blamed' for failing to reject any associations with all-things Russian and/or Soviet. On the contrary, this viewpoint stresses the idea that 'western' Ukrainians also need to better understand eastern Ukraine's historical interactions with Russia as a state and Russians as a nation. In this way, such individuals are demonstrating that indeed monuments of Lenin are a part of 'their' history, part of the way they visualise 'where they are from' and in this way are fully justified.

> For only 60 years we have been a whole Ukraine and previously we were part of different territories. Therefore because of this, we are totally different people. People from western Ukraine come here and do not understand our mentality. Why don't we get rid of the monuments to Dzerzhinsky and Lenin? Why? It is because the monuments do not get in our way, they are a part of our history and why should we get rid of it?[258]

This was noted by Zhurzhenko, such individuals simply have a different historical perspective of what it means to be Ukrainian, than people in different parts of Ukraine.[259]

There was a second viewpoint which, whilst acknowledging the existence of such differences across Ukraine, saw them to a certain extent as being 'artificially constructed' by the media and political forces so as to legitimate their own political ends:

> I think that this idea about the differences between East and West Ukraine is thought up *naddumanni* (a little far-fetched). It happened in the Soviet period, when

---

258 Natal'ya, assistant lecturer, Luhans'k Taras Shevchenko State Pedagogical University, 24 February 2003.

259 Zhurzhenko, T., "The myth of two Ukraines", can be found at: www.eurozine.com, downloaded, 25 September 2004.

I was at school. We travelled to western Ukraine and they knew straightaway that we were from Donbas. We don't speak the Russian letter 'g' we speak *surzhyk*, using the letter 'h' instead! We got a boy in our class who spoke Ukrainian well and clearly and asked the local people directions and they helped him because when we asked they gave us the wrong directions on purpose. Now this does not happen and there are more friendly relations. We have an exchange programme here in Lugansk, connected to the *Narodnyi Rukh*, who organise exchanges between eastern and western Ukraine.[260]

Indeed, many individuals strove to highlight the fact that in recent years, there has been much discussion of language politics in Ukraine, with people in eastern Ukraine gaining the impression that if they travelled to western Ukraine and spoke the Russian language, this would create tensions with the local population. As highlighted in the passage below, individuals were surprised upon travelling to western Ukraine to find that such a 'representation' of events was not in fact correct:

Yes, we were told that in L'viv, if you ask directions in Russian, then they would give you the wrong directions. This wasn't the case. If you speak with local people in Russian, they also will speak back in Russian so you can understand them. Maybe in some deep villages, where the level of civilisation is very low, then maybe this is the case, but I personally haven't encountered this.[261]

Moreover, many teachers spoke of successful exchanges between their cities and ones in western Ukraine, which in many ways greatly assisted in the breaking down of 'stereotypes' of people from the 'east' and the 'west' of Ukraine:

For four years in a row, the Luhans'k region team in the (Ukrainian) schools Olympics, have held close links with the L'viv team. The spectators were astounded, 'how is it that the most eastern and most western areas are friends'. Maybe this is more important than the actual results of the competition. The children have the skills to speak to each other, find a common language. These two teams are still

---

260   School history teacher, Luhans'k, 14 March 2003.
261   Tatyana, school history teacher, Kharkiv, 23 March 2003.

keeping in touch. I think that facts are facts, but it is important how you take them on and use them in history education.[262]

In particular, the importance of 'perceptions' of regional differences across Ukraine was outlined in the passage below:

> By the way, not long ago, I travelled on a train with a lady from L'viv. Her roots were from St. Petersburg. She said that in L'viv, there are Russian language schools in each *raion* (district). It is not true that there is taking place full measured Ukrainisation. I myself have been a few times to L'viv and spoke with people in Russian. And they answered my questions and helped me out. This is to say that we still have here in eastern Ukraine prejudice, strengthened by our old relations to western Ukraine.[263]

Whilst regional differences certainly exist between the western and eastern parts of Ukraine, for example, between the cities of L'viv and Luhans'k, such comments bear evidence to the significance of 'misperceptions' having the real potential of constantly reinforcing such differences in the eyes of the general population, making the task of the state to engineer an all-embracing Ukrainian identity even greater to achieve.

Turning attention to the schoolchildren, in a similar fashion to their teachers, many children stated how before actually travelling to western Ukraine, they had felt a degree of apprehension concerning their use of the Russian language:

> I was in the Carpathians not long ago and it is interesting to think about the relations between western and eastern Ukraine. We thought that they would call us *moskali*, but a man we met in L'viv, said that they only call *moskali*, those people who live in L'viv and speak Russian and that we shouldn't worry.[264]

Whilst this opinion was voiced on several occasions, many children expressed a negative representation of 'western' Ukraine, to a great degree, defined by its relation to the Russian language. As one Kharkiv schoolgirl notes, "Western Ukraine has a very negative attitude towards the Russian

---

262   Tatyana, school history teacher, Luhans'k, 25 April 2003.
263   Grigoriy, school history teacher, Luhans'k, 5 March 2003.

language. There it has been banned to listen to Russian music on public transport."[265] Many children expressed a dislike to such an open dislike of Russia, with 'western Ukraine' negatively perceived as the hotbed of Ukrainian nationalism; "Ukraine is made up of two parts, western and eastern Ukraine. Western Ukraine has a more sharp politics, she is against Russia. There should be a sensible nationalism, and not fanaticism."[266]

Western Ukraine was criticised not only for its dislike of the Russian language, but also for the fact that as a region of Ukraine, it has been 'polluted' by foreign neighbouring countries, in the most part Poland. As Artem, a schoolboy in Kharkiv, notes, "We have differences between the western and eastern parts. In the western part they don't speak the Ukrainian language, they speak Polish combined with Ukrainian."[267]

> Lots of people in western Ukraine think that they are more Ukrainian than we are as they speak Ukrainian. Yet their culture is a mix of Polish and Ukrainian cultures. They have Catholic churches, it is not pure Ukrainian culture, and it is very mixed. All they have is their language. To hear real Ukrainian, you must go to Poltava Oblast.[268]

Many individuals spoke of how people in 'western' Ukraine saw themselves as 'more' Ukrainian on the basis of language use, than 'eastern' Ukrainians. As one schoolgirl in Luhans'k states, "They think that they are real Ukrainians and we are Russians. I disagree. I am Ukrainian, I was born in this country and I live in this country. It doesn't matter what language you speak."[269]

> In the eastern part of Ukraine, we don't have clean Ukrainian, we have a Russian accent. And in western Ukraine, they have strong Czech and Polish influences. When I was in western Ukraine, they say that they are real Ukrainians. I don't think that it is true because they have lots of Polish culture in western Ukraine. I think that

264   Schoolboy, Sumy, 14 March 2003.
265   Schoolgirl, Kharkiv, 4 April 2003.
266   Schoolboy, Kharkiv, 4 April 2003.
267   Schoolboy, Kharkiv, 19 March 2003.
268   Ibid.
269   Schoolgirl, Luhans'k, 14 March 2003.

now we have to build our nation from the very beginning. We have to unite and to develop our different regions.[270]

Such responses reveal the way that attitudes to the Russian language shapes the identity of respondents, in particular, their awareness of regional diversity across Ukraine.

Such efforts to understand identity solely using a 'language' marker were, however, wholly rejected by the vast majority of the schoolchildren, with many individuals feeling such a view as deeply insulting:

> I think that this is stupid. We are one people, but history has turned out that western Ukraine and eastern Ukraine are against each other. This is not clever. We are one country. Simply for us, Russian is as much 'our' language as Ukrainian is for people in western Ukraine. In western Ukraine, they have even tried to ban Russian language and because of this, there were many protests. We since birth have spoken Russian. And it turns out, that just because of this, that we speak Russian and not because of other reasons, such a love for Russia or personal convictions, they in western Ukraine consider that we are *chuzhyi* 'foreign' people, although we live in one country.[271]

The underlying message which emerged was that many schoolchildren in Ukraine's eastern borderlands felt that they were 'misrepresented' with commentators making the bold jumps in logic that on account of speaking the Russian language, people in eastern Ukraine were 'Russian-loving' and simultaneously deeply sceptical of Ukraine as an independent state. As a boy in Luhans'k claimed, "We are just the same Ukrainians as they are, we are one nation, one country."[272] Many children wanted to express the view that they were Ukrainian and were proud of this. Whilst they spoke the Russian language, they did not consider this to make them less a 'Ukrainian'; rather they defined their identities using markers other than solely language usage.

---

270   Schoolgirl, Luhans'k, 14 March 2003.
271   Schoolboy, Luhans'k, 5 March 2003.
272   Schoolboy, Luhans'k, 14 February 2003.

5.3   Reflections on 'Russia' as Ukraine's 'other'

This section centres on how Russia and Russians are perceived by individuals in the three study areas.

5.3.1 The Russian-Ukrainian border

While engaging with issues surrounding regionalism in Ukraine, it is
useful to consider that patterns of regional and national identities often do not
coincide with state borders. All three of the study areas are situated adjacent
to the Russian-Ukrainian state border and thus may be open to the forces of
'transnational regionalism.'[273] In particular, as a result of Ukraine's historical
closeness with Russia, individuals may still identify with people living on the
other side of the border in 'foreign' territory.

Concerning opinions of the older generation, there was a near or total
consensus of disapproval of the need for such a border. Many respondents
stated that there was simply no need to make such a symbolic demarcation
where in reality no divisions actually existed. A common view is illustrated in
the following remark: "For us it is not necessary to strengthen the border. On
the contrary, the border needs to be opened. The majority of my relatives live
in Russia. For us, it will be a tragedy if a visa regime is installed with external
passports."[274] Indeed, the real consequences of the border being imple-
mented are highlighted by the laments of an educational methodologist in
Luhans'k, who tells of her family, now living on both sides of the Russian-
Ukrainian border:

> My husband is from Chertkova (border crossing) in Russia but my niece got married
> in Milovoye in Ukraine but her parents still live in Chertkova. We go to visit them
> and give her a chicken and some sour cream and then on the border crossing they
> ask her where are you taking this food? Is the border necessary for her? There eve-
> rything is *rodnoi* (native).[275]

---

273   Hurrell, A., "Explaining the resurgence of Regionalism in World Politics", *Review of
       International Studies*, 21, 4, October 1995: 333.
274   Natal'ya, assistant lecturer, Luhans'k Taras Shevchenko State Pedagogical
       University, 12 March 2003.
275   Olga, former teacher trainer in history, Institute of Uninterrupted Education,
       Luhans'k Oblast, 12 March 2003.

Whilst amongst the older generation there was agreement on this issue, amongst the younger generation this issue proved more controversial. One school of thought emerged which repeated the stance of the older generation, arguing that the border serves no purpose as they see no divisions between Ukraine and Russia. Such a viewpoint is illustrated in the following two passages by schoolchildren from two different schools: "Over the centuries, Belarus, Ukraine and Russia have lived together, then they abruptly split up. But we don't see any borders between ourselves. We were always one family and remain so today."[276]

Furthermore, another schoolboy states, "They are 'our' people, Slavic people. It is our nation, Belarus, Russia and Ukraine – it is a Slavic nation.[277]

However, there also existed an opposing viewpoint which argued that the border was necessary on the basis of preserving Ukraine's territorial integrity. As one schoolboy states: "We cannot just get rid of the border with Russia because Ukraine is a smaller state and if we rejoin with Russia, Ukraine will lose its nationality and Russia would be left as a unitary state."[278] Such comments were repeated in numerous interviews. Here, individuals were expressing a fear that if the border was allowed to disappear, this would certainly hinder Ukraine, allowing Russia to take control over Ukraine. For these schoolchildren, the border symbolised a necessary defensive 'tool', used by Ukraine to preserve its state independence. Regarding the importance of the border, one can state that whilst for the older generation, who were educated and worked for the majority of their lives in the Soviet Union, there was no 'physical' border between the two countries and for them the border has no relevance, other than being a hindrance.

For the younger generation, the issue is more hotly disputed. Here, one can witness to a certain degree the results of the Ukrainian state's efforts to re(engineer) a sense of Ukrainian identity. These schoolchildren have spent their entire formative years within independent Ukraine and have a greater sense of where 'our' territory ends and where the 'other' begins. The negotiation of the issue of the border demonstrates that in this new generation a sense of territorial identity, feelings of being part of a political entity, Ukraine,

---

276   Schoolboy, Kharkiv, 4 April 2003.
277   Schoolboy, Kharkiv, 19 March 2003.
278   Schoolboy, Luhans'k, 26 February 2003.

which has clear demarcated boundaries, is slowly emerging. Such results add substance to the argument that over time, generational differences will emerge in Ukraine and necessarily a more homogenous population will form as more and more people are educated in the independent Ukrainian state.

5.3.2 Russian-Ukrainian relations

Concerning general relations between Russia and Ukraine, from the interviews with the older generation emerged a dislike of efforts to 'artificially' divide Ukraine and Russia. As one school history teacher in Kharkiv states:

> Definite political forces are interested in breaking ties between Russia and Ukraine. They try to erect some sort of barrier. But for many centuries, both our peoples have had single roots, everything was inter-connected, and artificially to break these connections is not possible. All the more, in the world at present is taking place processes of integration. And what will we, as Slavic nations, break apart? History will not allow this.[279]

Many respondents voiced such an opinion, seeing attempts to represent Russia as an 'other' in a perennial negative light, artificial and ultimately self-defeating. Of particular relevance here, many individuals expressed the opinion that if any 'other' needed to be defined for people in eastern Ukraine, then in place of 'Russia', 'western Ukraine' was closer to the mark:

> We don't have a clear picture of 'we are khokhli and they are moskali.' We look onto Russia in a normal fashion, like towards a neighbour. More often we can hear, 'we are from Eastern Ukraine' and 'they' are Banderites and nationalists. Although our population is very apathetic. Western Ukraine is closer to the western countries and they have a mentality of the individual, which is more developed. Here, in eastern Ukraine, we have influences from Asia and Russia. At the everyday level, we have greater problems with relations with western Ukraine than with Russia. In eastern Ukraine, nobody is bothered if you are Russian or Ukrainian, we all speak the Russian language.[280]

In this way, individuals were demonstrating that for them, there were no boundaries between them and Russians living on the other side of the border,

---

279   Anatoliy, reader in pedagogy, 22 March 2003.
280   Teacher, Sumy, 10 April 2003.

with internal regional differences across Ukraine seen as more relevant. Furthermore, it is interesting to witness the 'language issue' again being used as a legitimating tool in this argument. This again provides evidence of the way that divisions in Ukraine, cannot be simplistically put down to single factors, such as language or ethnicity or region. Instead, these identity markers overlap and crosscut continually.

Turning to the reflections of the schoolchildren, here the issue proved highly contested. One viewpoint reiterated that of the older generation, seeing Ukraine and Russia as occupying one, single cultural, political space and thus there was simply no need to 'create' boundaries, where none were necessary. As a schoolgirl states, "Ukraine and Russia are two sisters and their people are brothers. The relations of Russians to Ukrainians and vice versa is friendly, and even when we hear something negative about Russia, we worry. They are not foreigners."[281] Moreover, holders of such an opinion explained their dislike of Russia and Russians being continually represented in a negative light. As a schoolboy states, whilst he accepts that Ukrainians were oppressed during the Soviet times, this for him does not equate to a justification to hate Russians as a nation *per se*; "We have to develop friendly relations with Russia because it is our neighbour, they are Slavic people, the people are not to blame for the fact that in Soviet times someone in Moscow oppressed the Ukrainians."[282] Furthermore, such negative attitudes are understood as 'created artificially' by political elites who want to impose 'their' own understanding of Ukraine's relations towards Russia, a relationship which many schoolchildren view as unnecessary, overtly nationalist and divergent from their own viewpoint. As Zhenya, a schoolgirl from Kharkiv notes:

> About the question whether to go to Europe or Russia, I think that we should turn to Russia. I think that Russia could be even better than Europe; it has a great potential no European country can compete with Russia. In culture and religion, we are almost the same as Russia. The big problem is now there are some nationalists in

281 Schoolgirl, Kharkiv, 3 April 2003.
282 Schoolboy, Luhans'k, 14 February 2003.

our politics and these angry people will make big problems in our relations with Russia. They want to be separate from Russia, but we should be together. [283]

Here again emerges a certain sense of frustration that 'their' voice is not being heard, drowned out by 'nationalist' interpretations of Russian-Ukrainian relations. Whilst strong emotions emerged in support of maintaining close ties with Russia, there also emerged a discourse amongst the schoolchildren which again demonstrated an emerging territorial Ukrainian identity, rejecting overtures to rejoin with Russia, as a schoolgirl states: "Uniting with Russia will be negative, especially concerning the national question, Ukrainians would lose their national pride, traditions, language."[284] In particular, individuals argued that Ukraine 'needed to stand up on her own two feet', and cease to regard Russia as an 'elder' brother, with 'special' status in Ukrainian political and societal life. This is highlighted in the following passage:

It is not important what sort of relations we have with Russia. She is not a 'special' country for Ukraine. Yes, we were once part of Russia, but we were also part of the USSR, where there were many other different countries. I think that there shouldn't be any special relations with Russia. She is only one of the countries, which Ukraine should cooperate with.[285]

Amongst this younger generation there was a real understanding and awareness of the fact that they were growing up in a rapidly changing world, one in which Ukraine, as an independent country in her own right, certainly had a large role to play. As one girl succinctly sums up, "We were born in the USSR, but we were not conscious about life. But we have grown up and been educated in Ukraine. And Russia for us is already a different country."[286]

---

283   Zhenya, schoolgirl, Kharkiv, 19 March 2003.
284   Zhenya, schoolgirl, Kharkiv, 19 March 2003.
285   Schoolgirl, Kharkiv, 4 April 2003.
286   Schoolgirl, Kharkiv, 4 April 2003.

5.4   Conclusions

This chapter has shed light on two main areas: understandings of the importance of the 'regional' factor in the politics of identity in Ukraine, and representations of Russia as Ukraine's 'other'. Regarding the regional textbooks, it was found that in the case of Luhans'k and Kharkiv, regional elites were attempting to create an 'alternative' version of historical events to the 'official' state narrative, involving a 'softer' line towards Russia and Russians. Here, the rhetoric shifts from a tone of 'blame' and 'negation' to a celebration of 'mutual understanding' and 'peaceful interaction'. In Sumy, there was scant attention paid to such issues, which one can conclude to reflect an implicit acceptance by Sumy's elites of the 'official' narrative and also a result of Sumy's greater political passivity compared to the other two study areas. This demonstrates the existence of clear regional differences within 'Eastern Ukraine'.

Concerning reflections on the issue of 'regionalism' at the local level, both generations, young and old, expressed an understanding of the regional differences across Ukraine, with differences between the 'east' and the 'west' receiving much attention. This demonstrates the fact that subjective and objective markers of regions across Ukraine do not coincide. Whilst the 8-10 classification system which was described in Chapter 2 is an extremely useful analytical tool for outlining the objective regional differences across Ukraine, it is certainly relevant to witness how individual perceptions of Ukraine's regional diversity are far different. In Ukraine's eastern borderlands, at the grassroots level, a simplistic division of Ukraine is constructed into 'western' and 'eastern' halves, with the 'Eastern Ukraine' identity held onto as a certain 'barrier' to the perceived negative influence of 'Western Ukraine' in the government based in Kiev.

The results from this empirical research highlight that individuals in these three study areas had a clear understanding of 'who they were' and were highly involved in the politics of identity in Ukraine, desiring 'their voice to be heard'. Many felt disillusioned towards the political process which they felt did not represent their views. Many individuals expressed a dislike at being classified as 'bad' Ukrainians on account of speaking the Russian language and holding sympathetic views towards Russia. Here, emerges a clear illustration of the way that 'regional' understandings of self-identification are implicitly mixed and blurred with linguistic identifications. Individuals in these 'eastern borderlands' felt 'no less' Ukrainian than Ukrainian-speakers from L'viv. Rather, 'Ukrainianness' is defined using a different set of markers.

Such ideas were also reflected in opinions regarding the state border with Russia and Russians as a people. Interestingly, amongst the older generation, there existed a determination to reject attempts to represent Russia as Ukraine's eternal 'other'. Whilst many schoolchildren also repeated such a viewpoint, significantly, there also emerged a distinct 'position', which felt that Ukraine needed to 'defend' its independent status, and a delineated border was the necessary means of achieving this. Many schoolchildren expressed a view that re-joining with Russia would be a tragedy for Ukraine and its people, allowing Russia to once again control Ukraine for her own ends. Whilst such ideas reflect a growing sense of difference and 'otherness' towards the Russian *state,* nevertheless, schoolchildren were keen to demonstrate how they still desired close and friendly relations with their Russian neighbours.

6   Conclusions: Key Empirical Findings

This study has approached the task of examining the politics of identity in Ukraine by asking three overarching questions. Regarding the first question, 'Where are we from?' the study has investigated how 'historical' identities are affecting wider national identities across Ukraine. The second question, 'Where are we?' has necessitated a thorough examination of the importance of the 'regional' factor within processes of identity change. The third question, 'Who we are not?' has sought to explore to what extent Russia is perceived as Ukraine's real 'other'.

This study has critically engaged with the literature regarding the 'mapping' of identities. In Chapter 1, it was demonstrated that whilst much academic rigour has devoted itself to examining ethnic and linguistic differences across Ukraine, assumptions about their significance have been misplaced. Instead, the study calls for a deeper engagement with the relevance of the 'regional' factor in the politics of identity in Ukraine and Chapter 2 devoted itself to this issue, providing a framework in which such 'meta-regions' can be deconstructed. The study chose to deconstruct the term 'Eastern Ukraine' by focusing attention on the eastern borderlands of Ukraine. In this manner, the study has provided a clear 'regional' framework through which identity change can be analysed at a number of different sites and levels.

To answer the first question, *'Where are we from?'* Chapter 3 focused on how the Ukrainian state has revised the historical narrative taught in schools. By analysing school history textbooks, it was found that the Ukrainian state is actively engaged in the politics of national identity, continually focusing attention on the longevity of the Ukrainian nation and its eternal struggle for state independence. Formally, the state has total control over the contents of these textbooks and their publishing, thus creating the possibility to create 'one' historical narrative, taught across the whole of Ukraine. However, this research uncovered the beginnings of a *regional politics of the textbook*, in which publishing houses, located in various regional centres published textbooks with alternative interpretations of Ukraine's history. Thus, on the one hand, the state is 'formally' espousing the need for one overarching historical narrative to be used across the whole of Ukraine aimed at uniting the population. At the same time, it is implicitly allowing regional interpretations to emerge and be utilised in the Ukrainian classroom thus rendering the possibility that the status quo in terms of regional diversity may continue.

Chapter 4 engaged with how the revised 'historical narrative' was negotiated in the study areas. The results demonstrated that school history teachers were not implicit 'transmitters' of knowledge from the state to its citizenry, but 'active' players. Many of these individuals had been educated and trained in the Soviet system and taught the previous Soviet historical narrative, which celebrated the 'eternal union' of the Russian and Ukrainian peoples. Today, they are teaching a new, revised historical narrative, which rejects previous Soviet interpretations. Teachers whilst finding this process arduous, nevertheless were in full agreement of the need for Ukraine's children to learn a 'real' history about their country and learn 'where they were from' and at the same time, were in full understanding of the role of the 'History of Ukraine' course as a key state 'tool' aimed at (re)fashioning national identities. This support for the current reforms, however, was dampened by anxieties concerning some of the elements in the new narrative, which were deemed nationalistic.

In particular, two events deserve special mention; the Famine of 1932/3 and the War years of 1941/4. Many teachers expressed concerns that the interpretation in the textbooks regarding the Famine was overtly 'negative', with blame being placed wholly at the feet of the 'Russian' government. Similarly regarding the War years, many individuals expressed concerns that the Ukrainian state was trying to dispense with the Soviet-era understanding of the war with Nazi Germany as the 'Great Patriotic War'. The actions of the OUN/UPA also created heated debates. Whilst teachers were in full agreement that all the activities, which took place in the war years across Ukraine, should be discussed and in the history textbooks, many individuals felt that the new state narrative had taken an unnecessary slant towards trying to 'rehabilitate' the OUN/UPA movement and portray them as 'Ukrainian freedom-fighters'. Of particular note here, the issue of 'perception' is deemed extremely relevant. Many individuals were deeply critical of the 'nationalistic' and 'pro-Banderite' slant of the new textbooks, however such exclamations did not fully coincide with the reality of the contents of the textbooks. As outlined in Chapter 3, there was an appraisal of events in Ukraine in the war years, yet this appraisal was far from being unduly 'one-sided' and 'nationalistic' in content. Here, seemingly one can witness 'perceptions' of what is happening in the sphere of historical education which do not match with actual realities, with such misinterpretations, fuelled by existing 'regional stereotypes' of these historical events and figures. In Ukraine's eastern borderlands, there exists a particular 'regional' interpretation of these events, which is very close to previous Soviet interpretations.

In general, schoolteachers were concerned about the overtly 'negative' representation of all things Russian and Soviet. Many individuals expressed concerns that the fundamental aims of historical education was to unite the population of Ukraine, yet such 'negativity' had the danger of further deepening existing divisions. As a reaction to such changes, certain individuals implicitly stated how, rather than openly rejecting the state message, they instead chose to subtly 'pick and choose' the accent they gave to certain historical events. This phenomenon of selective appropriation of 'messages' can be described as 'inclusion without exclusion'. In this manner, the author concludes that it is clearly possible that teachers, acting as rational individual actors, play a highly significant role in the process of identity change, having the possibility rather than simply 'transferring' the state message to the schoolchildren, of adapting it to suit particular 'regional' interpretations of disputed historical events or figures.

Thus, the emergence of a paradoxical interplay between top-down processes is witnessed, in which efforts are being made to 'unite' the population using a single, historical narrative, and bottom-up processes, in which this message is being contested and adapted so as to reflect a specific 'regional' understanding of Ukraine's past. It was found that teachers chose to contest the state narrative as they felt that the 'nationalist' and 'anti-Russia' undertones of the new, state narrative were the product of 'western Ukrainian nationalists' influence in Kiev. As a reaction to this current situation, many individuals were keen to express the 'regional' differences across Ukraine and also exalt their endorsement of an 'East Ukrainian' regional identity, which rejected attempts to portray Russia as the 'other' in Ukraine's identity politics, instead seeing 'Western Ukraine' as the real 'other'.

Turning to the schoolchildren, rather than being 'passive' recipients of the state's historical message, they were engaged in the politics of identity. Regarding all the key historical events and figures, schoolchildren demonstrated differing interpretations on all of them, as highlighted in Chapter 4. An emerging division in the understanding of history is clearly visible between the events studied before and during the twentieth century. Regarding pretwentieth century history, the state's historical narrative was generally accepted.

However, in respect of history taught in the twentieth century, many children spoke of the influence of their parents and relatives. They often found it difficult to judge which historical narrative to accept, the state's version taught at school, or an alternative version, told by their parents and relatives. The Famine and the War years of 1941/44, provoked the greatest amount of debate with many schoolchildren reinforcing the 'Soviet' interpretation of OUN/UPA as 'traitors', whilst at the same time, rejecting attempts to portray Russia as Ukraine's 'other'. Children expressed a great desire to learn about 'where they are from', yet not at the expense of accepting an overtly negative historical narrative. Here, whilst generational differences are seen to exist with the younger generation more willing to embrace the new Ukrainian historical narrative, such differences are not clear-cut. Results in this study demonstrate that 'Soviet era' memories are not totally rejected by the younger generation. This seemingly proves the life experiences of families, including parents and grandparents have a profound impact on their children's understanding and interpretations of the Soviet past and *per se* demonstrates the enduring resonance of 'Soviet' understandings of Ukraine's historical development, which are passed on from generation to generation in certain areas of Ukraine. Significantly many proponents of the state-led nation building project argue how over time, generational differences will inevitably emerge with younger Ukrainians, educated in an independent Ukrainian state holding increasingly 'pro-Ukrainian' viewpoints than members of older generations. However, the results of this research demonstrate that such a prediction is only one of the likely outcome scenarios. Evidence here highlights how young people in these areas of Ukraine's eastern borderlands, in many respects are choosing to take on board parts of the nation building project which they like, whilst rejecting other areas which they dislike, in a similar fashion to older members of society and so specific 'regional' understandings of questions such as 'what it means to be Ukrainian?' are to an extent being replicated, making the state's efforts to create a homogenous population extremely arduous.

Turning attention to the second question of *'Where are we?'*, and the importance of the 'region' in the politics of identity in Ukraine, the analysis of 'regional' textbooks indicated that the local authorities were actively involved in this key area of identity change. In Kharkiv and Luhans'k the 'regional' textbooks certainly provided a *competing* narrative to the all-Ukrainian textbooks. Whilst Chapter 3 had concluded that the Ukrainian state was endeavouring to glorify the antiquity of the Ukrainian nation and state representing Russia as a clear 'other' for Ukraine, in Luhans'k and Kharkiv, much attention was placed on highlighting the joint settlement and co-operation between the Russian and Ukrainian peoples of these areas and also legitimating the continued use of the Russian language. In contrast, in Sumy, the lack of any real engagement with such issues can be read as an implicit acceptance of the all-Ukrainian historical narrative and demonstrates the inherent differences of this area from Kharkiv and Luhans'k and as such the existence of regional diversity within 'Eastern Ukraine'. From such results, the use of in-depth qualitative research is justified, uncovering nuances, which quantitative research may have failed to uncover.

The empirical findings from Chapter 5 highlight that individuals living in the eastern borderlands have a clear 'regional' understanding of their place in Ukraine. Many individuals were keen to express the differences, which exist across Ukraine, often comparing 'eastern' and 'western' parts of Ukraine. Many individuals expressed deep regret that 'eastern Ukraine' was stereotyped as 'pro-Russian and sometimes anti-Ukrainian' solely because of the use of the Russian language there. Here the actual crosscutting nature of 'regional' and 'linguistic' identities in Ukraine is witnessed. Many individuals spoke about how much rhetoric from western Ukraine represented 'eastern Ukraine' as 'less Ukrainian' than 'western Ukraine' on account of the wide usage of the Russian language in the eastern regions of the country. However, individuals rejected this view, arguing that whilst people used the

Russian language this did not automatically correspond to 'being less Ukrainian'. Implicitly, many individuals were demonstrating the multiplicity and diversity of ways how individuals define their national identities across Ukraine.

Finally, the third question which this study has sought to address is 'Who are we not?' To answer this question, attention has been placed on the state's attempts to represent Russia as the real 'other' for Ukraine and also individuals' own reflections on this issue. As demonstrated in Chapter 3, the Ukrainian state has made a clear attempt to represent Russia as Ukraine's 'other' in the revised historical narrative, now taught in Ukrainian schools. In Chapter 5, individuals were encouraged to discuss two separate themes, namely the Russian-Ukrainian state border and more generally Russian-Ukrainian relations. Concerning thoughts about the Russian-Ukrainian border, the majority of respondents did not see any need for a border to exist, seeing instead the border as a physical hindrance to their daily lives, often prohibiting individuals visiting their relatives living on the other side of the border in Russia. This was particularly the case amongst the interviewees of older generations. These people, who have spent the formulative years of their lives living in the 'multinational' Soviet state, clearly find it extremely difficult to comprehend the necessity for a physical delineation between Russia and Ukraine. These results indicate that there is the possibility of 'transnational regionalism' existing in these areas which may hamper the overall aims of the Ukrainian state.

However, the results of interviews with schoolchildren show that in this younger generation, there is more support for the state border. This demonstrates the effects of the Ukrainian state's attempts to engender an increased sense of national consciousness since 1991. These schoolchildren, aged between fifteen and seventeen years old, are the first generation of children to have been educated solely in an independent Ukrainian state and from these results, a gradual growth is witnessed in the sense of 'territorial' identification with the Ukrainian state. Concerning general reflections on Russia, many individuals of the older generation were wary of seeing Russia as an 'other', arguing that whilst Ukraine needed to find its own place in the world, this did not necessarily mean a total rejection of links with Russia. Many schoolchildren agreed with such a viewpoint, yet there were also other 'voices' who clearly viewed Russia as an 'other', expressing a desire for Ukraine to move away from Russia's influence. Again, such results can be seen as a 'measured' success of the state's nation building efforts. Even though many schoolchildren were wary about the Russian *state*, nevertheless, they desired close and amicable relations with their Russian neighbours at the everyday, local level. The author concludes that in Ukraine's eastern borderlands, whilst there have been some shifts in terms of territorial identity, especially amongst the younger generation, Russia is far from being perceived as a real 'other'. Instead, as highlighted in Chapter 5, when pressed on the issue of 'otherness' in Ukraine's internal politics of identity, many individuals felt that 'western' Ukraine was much more of an 'other' than Russia.

Overall the study has provided a 'regional' framework through which identity change in Ukraine can be gauged. By 'deconstructing' the meta-definitions in this instance 'eastern Ukraine' and conducting research at the micro-level at three different study areas within Ukraine's eastern borderlands, the study has revealed local responses and negotiation of wider processes of identity change.

Finally, since this research was undertaken, the presidential elections of 2004 in Ukraine, the 'Orange Revolution' and the subsequent parliamentary elections in both 2006 and 2007 have all taken place. During this time the stereotypical view of Ukraine as a country inherently 'divided' between 'East' and 'West' has re(emerged) to become a popular explanation for political events in Ukraine. The results of the above events have again clearly highlighted the relevance of the regional factor in Ukrainian politics and society. However, in this study, the author has outlined the necessity for academics, policymakers and indeed politicians to veer away from this simplistic 'West versus East' divide. Rather, the author has advocated an analysis of Ukraine's unique brand of regionalism not in terms of divisions, but rather in terms of regional differences and diversity.

As the results of the empirical chapters highlight, in Ukraine's eastern borderlands, people are still highly sceptical of fully embracing the Ukrainian state-led nation-building project. One of the reasons for this is that in these areas, the Soviet era understanding of terms such as 'nationalism' still holds negative connotations. These anxieties were exploited by certain political forces in the run-up to the 2004 presidential elections. Yushchenko's representation as a nationalist greatly diminished his support in these areas, even though he was actually born in Sumy oblast. Also, as the findings of this study ably demonstrate, individuals in Ukraine's eastern borderlands see no reason for Russia to be represented as an 'other' and to a certain degree are willing to resist attempts of the Ukrainian state to distance itself from Russia. This again can be seen as a reason for the lack of support for Yushchenko in oblasts such as Luhans'k and Donets'k and conversely support for Yanokovych, who advocated close ties between Russia and Ukraine.

The results of this study show that many people in these regions are not overly supportive of state-led nation building projects and attempts to move towards Europe and simultaneously away from Russia. However, at the same time, there are no open protests either. Individuals in the study areas want to take part in the nation-building project, yet reject any attempts to wholly negate their region's specific historical and cultural links with Russia. The extent to which the Ukrainian state can create "unity out of diversity", accommodating desires to "Europeanise" Ukraine with simultaneous desires to maintain close links with Russia, remains one of the central tasks of the Kiev administration and main points of debate within Ukrainian political and societal life.

Bibliography

English Language Sources

Abdewal, R., "Memories of nations and states: Institutional history and national identity in Post-Soviet Eurasia", *Nationalities Papers*, 30, 3, 2002: 459-484.

Alexander, R.J., Versions of Primary Education, London: Routledge, 1995.

Anderson, B., *Imagined Communities: Reflections on the Origin and Spread of Nationalism*, London: Verso, 1991.

Apple, M.W. and Christian-Smith, *The Politics of the Textbook*, New York: Routledge, 1991.

Arel, D., *Language and the Politics of Ethnicity: The Case of Ukraine*, University of Illinois, (PhD dissertation), 1993.

Arel, D., "Language Politics in Independent Ukraine: Towards One or Two State Langauges?", *Nationalities Papers*, 23, 3, September 1995: 597-622.

Arel, D., "The Temptation of the Nationalising State", in Tismaneanu, V., (ed.), *Political Culture and Civil Society in Russia and the New States of Eurasia*, Armonk, NY: M.E. Sharpe 1995.

Arel, D. and Khmelko, V., "The Russian Factor and Territorial Polarisation in Ukraine", *Harriman Review*, 9, 1-2, 1996: 81-91.

Arel, D. and Wilson, A., "The Ukrainian parliamentary elections", *RFE/RL Research Report*, 3, 26, 1 July, 1994: 6-17.

Arel, D. and Wilson, A., "Ukraine: Back to Eurasia?", *RFE/RL ResearchReport*, 5, 32, 19 August 1994.

Barrington, L.W., "Region, Language, and Nationality: Rethinking Support in Ukraine for Maintaining Distance from Russia", in Kuzio, T. and D'Anieri, P., (eds.), *Dilemmas of State-Led Nation Building in Ukraine*, Westport, CT: Praeger, 2002: 131-146.

Barrington, L.W. and Herron, E.S., "One Ukraine or many? Regionalism in Ukraine and its Political Consequences", *Nationalities Papers*, 32, 1, March 2004: 53-86.

Batt, J., "Transcarpathia: Peripheral Region at the 'Centre of Europe'", in Batt, J. and Wolczuk, K., (eds.), *Regions, State and Identity in Central and Eastern Europe*, London and Portland, OR: Frank Cass, 2002.

Berlak. A and Berlak, H., *Dilemmas of Schooling: teaching and social change*, London, Methuen, 1981.

Bhabha, H., (ed.), *Nation and Narration*, London: Routledge, 1990.

Bibo, I., "The Distress of the East European Small States", in Nagy, K., (ed.), *Democracy, Revolution and Self-Determination: Selected Writings of Istvan Bibo*, Boulder, CO: Social Science Monographs, 1991.

Bilaniuk, L., "Speaking of Surzhyk: Ideologies and Mixed Languages", *Harvard Ukrainian Studies*, XXI, 1-2, June 1997: 93-118.

Birch, S., "Party System Formation and Voting Behaviour in the Ukrainian Parliamentary Elections of 1994", in Kuzio, T., (ed.), *Contemporary Ukraine: Dynamics of Post-Soviet Transformation*, Armonk, NY: M.E. Sharpe, 1998: 139-160.

Birch, S., "Interpreting the Regional Effect in Ukrainian Politics", *Europe-Asia Studies*, 52, 6, September 2000: 1017-1042.

Birch, S., *Elections and Democratisation in Ukraine*, London: MacMillan, 2000.

Birch, S. and Zinko, I., "The dilemmas of regionalism", *Transition*, November 1998: 22-25.

Bojcun, M., "The Ukrainian Parliamentary Elections in March-April 1994", *Europe-Asia Studies*, 47, 2, March 1995: 29-249.

Bourdieu, P., "Systems of Education and Systems of Thought", *International Social Science Journal*, 19, 3, 1967: 338-358.

Bourdieu, P., "Rethinking the State: Genesis and Structure of the Bureaucratic Field", *Sociological Theory*, 12,1, 1994.

Bradshaw, M. and Makarychev, A., "Globalization and Fragmentation: The Impact of the International Relations of Russia's Regions," in Ruble, B., Koehn, J. and Popson, N., (eds.), *Fragmented Spaces in the Russian Federation*, Washington DC: Woodrow Wilson Center Press, 2001.

Breuilly, J., Nationalism and the State, Manchester: Manchester University Press, 1993.

Bremmer, I., "The politics of ethnicity: Russians in the New Ukraine", *Europe-Asia Studies*, 46, 2, March/April 1994: 261-283.

Bromlei, I., (ed.), "Present-day Ethnic Processes in the USSR", *Progress*, Moscow, 1982: 414-452.

Brubaker, R., "Nationhood and the National Question in the Soviet Union and Post-Soviet Eurasia: An Institutionalist Account", *Theory and Society*, 23, 1, 47-78.

Bugajski, J., "Ethnic Relations and Regional Problems in Independent Ukraine", in Wolchik, S.L. and Zviglyanich, V., *Ukraine: The Search for a National Identity*, Lanham, MA: Rowman and Littlefield, 2000.

Burawoy, M. et al., *Ethnography Unbound*, Berkeley: University of California Press, 1991.

Clifford, J., "Diasporas", *Cultural Anthropology*, 9, 3, 1994.

Connor, W., *Ethnonationalism: The Quest for Understanding*, Princeton, NJ: Princeton University Press, 1994.

Conquest, R., *The Harvest of Sorrow: Soviet Collectivization and the Terror-Famine*, New York: Oxford University Press, 1986.

Craumer, P.R. and Clem, J.I., "Ukraine's emerging Electoral Geography: A Regional Analysis of the 1998 Parliamentary Elections", *Post-Soviet Geography and Economics*, 40, 1, 1999: 1-26.

Donnan, H. and Wilson, T.M., (eds,), *Border Approaches: Anthropological Perspectives on Frontiers*, Lanham, MA: University Press of America, 1994.

Durkheim, E., *Education and Sociology*, New York: Free Press, 1956.

Eley, G. and Suny, R.G., "Introduction: From the Moment of Social History to the Work of Cultural Representation", in their edited reader, *Becoming National*, New York: Oxford University Press, 1996: 3-38.

"Expert Assessments and Public Opinion Concerning the Border Policy of Ukraine", *Borders of Ukraine. Effective policy implementation*, Project of the Centre for Peace, Conversion and Foreign Policy of Ukraine, http://borders.Cpcfpu.org.ua/eng/analytics/index.shtml, accessed 29 April 2004.

Filippova, O., "Ukrainians and Russians in Eastern Ukraine: Ethnic Identity and Citizenship in the Light of Ukrainian Nation-Building", http://www.unl.ac.uk/ukrainecentre/WP/12.html, accessed 8 October 2001.

Flier, M.S., "Surzhyk: The Rules of Engagement", in Gitelman, Z., Hajda, L., Himka, J-P. and Solchanyk, R., *Cultures and Nations of Central and Eastern Europe, Essays in Honor of Roman Szporluk, Harvard Ukrainian Studies*, XXII, 1998.

Fournier, A., "Mapping Identities: Russian Resistance to Linguistic Ukrainisation in Central and Eastern Ukraine", *Europe-Asia Studies*, 54, 3, 2002: 416.

Franklin, S. and Shepard, J., *The Emergence of Rus 750-1200*, London: Longman, 1996.

Furrer, M., "National History and Exceptionality – the image of Switzerland as a country of exclusive fate in the light of changes in presenting this topic in school textbooks on history", in *Ukrains'ka Istorichna Dydaktika: Mizhnarodnyi Dialog*, Kiev: Geneza, 2000: 313-332.

Garnett, S.W., *Keystone in the Arch: Ukraine in the Emerging Security Architecture of Central and Eastern Europe*, Washington DC: Carnegie Endowment for International Peace, 1997.

Green, A., *Education, Globalization and the Nation-State*, Basingstoke: MacMillan Press, 1997.

Holdar, S., "Torn between East and West: The regional factor in Ukrainian politics", *Post-Soviet Geography*, 36, 2, February 1995: 112-132.

Hurrell, A., "Explaining the resurgence of regionalism in World Politics", *Review of International Studies*, 21, 4, October 1995.

Hutchinson, J., *The Dynamics of Cultural Nationalism*, London: Allen and Unwin, 1987.

Jackson, L., *The Construction of National Identity in Ukraine: A Regional Perspective*, PhD study, University of Birmingham, 1998.

Jackson, L., "Identity, Language and Transformation in Eastern Ukraine: A Case Study of Zaporizhzhia", in Kuzio, T., (ed.), *Contemporary Ukraine: Dynamics of Post-Soviet transformation*, Armonk, NY: M.E. Sharpe, 1998: 99-113.

Janmaat, J.G., "Language Politics in Education and the Response of the Russians in Ukraine", *Nationalities Papers*, 27, 3, 1999.

Janmaat, J.G., *Nation-Building in Post-Soviet Ukraine. Educational Policy and the Response of the Russian-Speaking Population*, Netherlands Geographical Society, 2000.

Jordan, G. and Weedon, C., *Cultural Politics, Class, Gender, Race and the Post-Modern World*, Oxford: Blackwell, 1995.

Jung, M., "The Donbas Factor in the Ukrainian Elections", *RFE/RL Research Report*, 25 March 1994: 52-53.

Kaiser, R., *The Geography of Nationalism in Russia and the USSR*, Princeton: Princeton University Press, 1983.

Kapferer, B., *Legends of People, Myths of State: Violence, Intolerance, and Political Culture in Sri Lanka and Australia*, Washington DC and London: Smithsonian Institution Press, 1988.

Keating, M., *Nations against the State: The new politics of nationalism in Quebec, Catalonia and Scotland*, Palgrave: New York, 2001.

Khmelko, V. and Arel, D., "The Russian Factor and Territorial Polarisation in Ukraine", *Harriman Review*, 9, 1-2, Spring 1996: 81-91.

Kolsto, P., *Nation-Building and Ethnic Integration in Post-Soviet Societies. An Investigation of Latvia and Kazakhstan*, Boulder, CO: Westview Press, 1999.

Krawchenko, B., *Social Change and National Consciousness in Twentieth Century Ukraine*, Basingstoke and London: Macmillan, 1985.

Kuromiya, H., *Freedom and Terror in the Donbas: A Ukrainian-Russian Borderland, 1870s-1990s*, Cambridge: Cambridge University Press, 1998.

Kuzio, T., *Ukraine: The Unfinished Revolution*, London: Alliance Publishers, 1992.

Kuzio, T., "National Identity in Independent Ukraine: An Identity in Transition", *Nationalism and Ethnic Politics*, 2, 4, 1996: 582-608.

Kuzio, T., *Ukraine: State and Nation Building*, London: Routledge, 1998.

Kuzio, T., "Election reveals Ukraine's geographic political divisions", *RFE/RL Newsline*, 6, 73, Part II, 18 April 2002.

Kuzio, T., "History, Memory and Nation Building in the Post-Soviet Colonial Space", *Nationalities Papers*, 30, 2, 2002: 241-264.

Kuzio, T., "The Nation-building Project in Ukraine and Identity: Toward a Consensus", in Kuzio, T. and D'Anieri, P., (eds.), *Dilemmas of State-Led Nation Building in Ukraine*, Westport, CT: Praeger, 2002.

Kuzio, T. and D'Anieri, P., (eds.), *Dilemmas of State-Led Nation Building in Ukraine*, Westport, CT: Praeger, 2002.

Laba, R., "The Russian-Ukrainian Conflict: State, Nation and Identity", *European Security*, 4, 3, 1995.

Laitin, D., *Identity in Formation: The Russian Speaking Populations in the Near Abroad*, Ithaca and London: Cornell University Press, 1998.

Leckey, C., "Provincial Readers and Agrarian Reform, 1760s-1770s: The Case of Sloboda Ukraine", *Russian Review*, 61, October 2002: 535-559.

Levinas, E., *The Levinas Reader*, Hand, S., (ed.), Oxford: Blackwell, 1989.

Liber, G., "Imagining Ukraine: regional differences and the emergence of an integrated state identity, 1926-1994", *Nations and Nationalism*, 4, 2, 1998: 187-206.

Lieven, A., *Ukraine and Russia: A fraternal rivalry*, Washington D.C: United States Institute of Peace Press, 1999.

Mace, J.E., "Famine and Nationalism in Soviet Ukraine", *Problems of Communism*, 33, 3, 1984: 37-50.

Magsoci, P.R., *A History of Ukraine*, Toronto: University of Toronto Press, 1996.

Marples, D.R. and Duke, D.F., "Ukraine, Russia and the Question of Crimea", *Nationalities Papers*, 23, 2, June 1995: 261-289.

McCrone, D., *The Sociology of Nationalism*, London: Routledge, 1998.

Meyer, D.J., "Why have Donbass Russians not ethnically mobilised like Crimean Russians have? An Institutional/Demographic Approach," in Micgiel D. J., (ed.), *State and Nation Building in East Central Europe: Contemporary Perspectives*, New York: Columbia University, 1996.

Miller, A.H., Klobucar, T.F., Reisinger, W.M. and Hesli, V.L., "Social Identities in Russia, Ukraine, and Lithuania", *Post-Soviet Affairs* 14, 1998: 248-286.

Morrison, J., "Pereyeslav and after: the Russian-Ukrainian Relationship", in *International Affairs*, 69, 4, 1993: 677-703.

Nahaylo, B., *The Ukrainian Resurgence*, London: Hurst, 1999.

National Ukrainian Census 2001: www.ukrcensus.gov.ua, accessed 29th April 2004.

Nemyria, G., "A Qualitative Analysis of the Situation in the Donbas", in Segbers, K. and De Spiegelaire, S., (eds.), *Emerging Geopolitical and Territorial Units. Theories, Methods and Case Studies. Post-Soviet Puzzles. Mapping the Political Economy of the Former Soviet Union*, vol.2, Baden and Baden: Nomos Verlagsgesellschaft, 1995: 57-58.

Nemyria, G., "Regionalism: An Underestimated Dimension of State-Building", in Wolchik, S.L. and Zviglyanich, V., (eds.), *Ukraine: The Search for a National Identity*, Lanham, MA: Rowman and Littlefield, 2000: 183-198.

Paasi, A., *Territories, Boundaries and Consciousness: The Changing Geographies of the Finnish-Russian Border*, New York: John Wiley, 1996.

Papadakis, Y., "Greek narratives of history and collective identity", *American Ethnologist*, 25, 2, May 1998: 149-165.

Piirainen, P., "The Fall of an Empire, the Birth of a Nation: Perceptions of the New Russian National Identity", in Chulos, C.J. and Piirainen, T., *The Fall of an Empire, the Birth of a Nation. National Identities in Russia*, Aldershot: Ashgate, 2000: 161-196.

Pilkington, H., *Russia's youth and its culture*, London: Routledge, 1994.

Pirie, P.S., "National Identity and Politics in Southern and Eastern Ukraine", *Europe-Asia Studies*, 48, 7, 1996: 1079-1104.

Plokhy, S., "The Ghosts of Pereyaslav: Russo-Ukrainian Historical Debates in the Post-Soviet Era", *Europe-Asia Studies*, 53, 3, 2001: 489-505.

Popson, N., "The Ukrainian History Textbook: Introducing Children to the 'Ukrainian nation' ", *Nationalities Papers*, 29, 2, 2001.

Popson, N., "Conclusion: Regionalism and Nation Building in a Divided Society", in Kuzio, T. and D'Anieri, P., (eds.), *Dilemmas of State-Led Nation Building in Ukraine*, Westport, CT: Praeger, 2002.

Prizel, I., *National Identity and Foreign Policy: Nationalism and Leadership in Poland, Russia and Ukraine*, Cambridge: Cambridge University Press, 1998.

Prymak, T., *Mykhailo Hrushevsky: The Politics of National Culture*, Toronto: University of Toronto Press, 1987.

Radcliffe, S. and Westwood, S., *Remaking the Nation: Place, Identity and Politics in Latin America*, London: Routledge, 1996.

Roper, S.D. and Fesnic, F., "Historical Legacies and their Impact on Post-Communist Voting Behaviour", *Europe-Asia Studies*, 55, 2003: 119-131.

Rose, R. and Haerpfner, C., *New Democracies Barometer V.A 12-Nation Survey*, Glasgow: Centre for the Study of Public Policy, University of Strathclyde, 1998.

Ryabchuk, M., "Civil Society and Nation Building in Ukraine", in Kuzio, T., (ed.), *Contemporary Ukraine: Dynamics of Post-Soviet Transformation*, Armonk, NY: M.E. Sharpe, 1998.

Ryabchuk, M., "A Future Ukraine: One Nation, Two Languages, Three Cultures?", *The Ukrainian Weekly*, 6 June 1999.

Ryabchuk, M., "Ambivalence to Ambiguity: Why Ukrainians remain unde-cided?", CERI-Sciences, April 2002.

Ryabchuk, M., "Culture and Cultural Politics in Ukraine: A Postcolonial Perspective", in Kuzio, T. and D'Anieri, P., (eds.), Dilemmas of State-Led Nation Building in Ukraine, Westport, CT: Praeger, 2002: 47-70.

Safran, W., "Diasporas in modern societies: Myths of Homeland and Return", Diaspora: A Journal of Transnational Studies, 1, 1, 1991.

Sahlins, P., Boundaries: The Making of France and Spain in the Pyrenees, Berkeley, CA: University of California Press, 1989.

Sasse, G., "The 'New' Ukraine: A State of Regions", Regional and Federal Studies, 11, Special Issue 3, Autumn 2001: 69-100.

Schlesinger, P., "On national identity: some conceptions and misconceptions criticized", Social Science Information 26, 2, 1987: 219-264.

Schweisfurth, M., Teachers, Democratisation and Educational Reform in Russia and South Africa, Oxford: Symposium Books, 2002.

Seely, R., "Ukraine's Identity Crisis", Moscow Times, 12 June 1994.

Shulga, N.A., "Ethnicity in Ukrainian Society as a Possible Source of Conflict", in Ehrhart, H. and Thranert, O., (eds.), European Conflicts and International Institutions: Cooperating with Ukraine, Baden-Baden: Nomos Verlagsgesell-schaft, 1998.

Shulman, S., "The cultural foundations of Ukrainian national identity", Ethnic and Racial Studies, 22, 6, November 1999: 1011-1036.

180   PETER W. RODGERS

Shulman, S., "The Internal-External Nexus in the Formation of Ukrainian National Identity: The Case for Slavic Integration", in Kuzio, T. and D'Anieri, P., *Dilemmas of State-led Nation Building in Ukraine*, Westport, CT: Praeger, 2002: 103-130.

Silver, B., "The ethnic and language dimensions in Russian and Soviet censuses", in Clem, R, (ed.), *Research Guide to the Russian and Soviet Censuses*, Ithaca: Cornell University Press, 1986: 70-97.

Simonsen, S.V., "Inheriting the Soviet policy toolbox: Russia's dilemma over ascriptive nationality", *Europe-Asia Studies*, 51, 6, 1999: 1069-87.

Smith, G., "The ethnic democracy study and the citizenship question in Estonia and Latvia", *Nationalities Papers*, 24, 2, 1996: 199-216.

Smith, G., "Post-Colonialism and Borderland Identities", in Smith, G. Vivien, L. Bohr, A. and Allworth, E., *Nation-Building in the Post-Soviet Borderlands. The Politics of National Identities*, Cambridge: Cambridge University Press, 1998: 1-20.

Snyder, T., *The Reconstruction of Nations. Poland, Ukraine, Lithuania, Belarus, 1569-1999*, London: Yale University Press, 2003.

Solchanyk, R., "The Politics of State Building: Centre-Periphery Relations in Post-Soviet Ukraine", *Europe-Asia Studies*, 46, 1, 1994: 42-68.

Solchanyk, R., *Ukraine and Russia: The Post-Soviet Transition*, Lanham, MA: Rowman and Littlefield, 2001.

Solonari, V., "Narrative, Identity, State: History Teaching in Moldova", *East European Politics and Societies*, 16, 2, 2002: 414-445.

Sovik, M., "Who am I? Perceptions of language and identity among students in Kharkiv", paper presented at a conference, organised by the Centre for Border Studies, at the University of Glamorgan, Pontypridd, entitled, 'Crossing Borders: History, Theories and Identities', 2-4 December, 2004.

Stepanenko, V., "Identities and Language Politics in Ukraine: The challenges of Nation-State Building", in Daftary, F. and Grin, F., (eds.), *Nation-Building, Ethnicity and Language Politics in Transition Countries*, Budapest: Open Society Institute, 2003 109-135.

Subtelny, O., *Ukraine: A History*, 2nd edition, Toronto: University of Toronto Press, 1992.

Sumy, Information can be found at http://online.sumy.ua/eng/history/ index.html, accessed 3 May 2004.

Szporluk, R., "Russians in Ukraine and Problems of Ukrainian Identity in the USSR", in Potichny, P.J., (ed.), *Ukraine in the 1970s*, Oakville, Ontario: Mosaic, 1975.

Szporluk, R., "The Soviet West-or Far Eastern Europe?", *East European Politics and Societies*, 5, 3, 1991: 466-482.

Szporluk, R., "Ukraine: From an Imperial Periphery to a Sovereign State", *Daedalus*, 126, 3, 1997: 85-119.

Todorov T., *"Mikhail Bakhtin: The Dialogical Principle"*, trans. by Godzich, W., Minneapolis: University of Minneapolis Press, 1984.

Tolz, V., "Forging the nation: National Identity and Nation Building in Post-Communist Russia", *Europe-Asia Studies*, 50, 6, 1998: 993-1022.

Triandafyllidou, A., "National Identity and the 'other'", *Ethnic and Racial Studies*, 21, 4, 1998: 593-612.

"Ukraine: The Birth and Possible Death of a Country", *The Economist*, 7 May 1994.

Ukraine's Central Elections Commission website, http://www.cvk.ukrpack.net, accessed 7 August 2002. Also: http://www.brama.com/ua-gov/el-94pre.html for the 1994 election results and http://www.skrobach.com/ukre1999.html. for the 1999 election results; both accessed 29 April 2004.

Velychenko, S., "The Official Soviet View of Ukrainian History", *Journal of Ukrainian Studies*, 10, 2, 1985.

Venezky, R., "Textbooks in School and Society", in Jackson, P.J., (ed.), *Handbook of Research and Curriculum*, New York: MacMillan, 1992.

Verdery, K., *National Identity under Socialism: Identity and Cultural Politics in Ceaucescu's Romania*, Berkeley, CA: University of California Press, 1995.

Von Hagen, M., "Does Ukraine have a History?", *Slavic Review*, 54, 3, 1995.

Wannner, C., "Historical narratives, Personal narratives: ethnographic perspectives on nation-ness in post-Soviet Ukraine", *Harriman Review*, 8, 2, Spring 1996: 11-15.

Wanner, C., *Burden of Dreams: History and Identity in Post-Soviet Ukraine*, University Park, PA: Pennsylvania University Press, 1998.

Williams, D. and Smith, R.J., "Dire U.S Forecast for Ukraine Conflict", *International Herald Tribune*, 26 January 1994.

Wilson, A., "The Growing Challenge to Kiev from the Donbas", *RFE/RL Research Report*, 20 August 1993.

Wilson, A., "The Donbas between Ukraine and Russia: The Use of History in Political Disputes", *Journal of Contemporary History*, London: SAGE Publications, 30, 1995: 265-289.

Wilson, A., "Myths of National History in Belarus and Ukraine", in Hosking, G. and Schopflin, G., (eds.), *Myths and Nationhood*, London: Hurst and Co, 1997: 182-197.

Wilson, A., *Ukrainian Nationalism in the 1990s: A Minority Faith*, Cambridge: Cambridge University Press, 1997.

Wilson, A., "Redefining ethnic and linguistic boundaries in Ukraine; indigenes, settlers and Russophone Ukrainians", in Smith, G. et al, *Nation-building in the Post-Soviet borderlands: The Politics of National Identity*, Cambridge: Cambridge University Press, 1998: 119-138.

Wilson, A., *The Ukrainians: unexpected nation*, New Haven: Yale University Press, 2000.

Wolczuk, K., "History, Europe and the 'National Idea': The 'Official' Narrative of National Identity Ukraine", *Nationalities Papers*, 28, 4, 2000: 671-694.

Wolczuk, K., "Catching up with 'Europe'? Constitutional Debates on the Territorial-Administrative Model in Independent Ukraine", Working Paper 2001, *One Europe or Several? Project.*

Wolczuk, K., "Conclusions: Identities, Regions and Europe", in Batt, J. and Wolczuk, K., (eds.), *Region, State and Identity in Central and Eastern Europe (The Case Series in regional and federal studies)*, London: Frank Cass, 2002.

Wolczuk, K., *The Moulding of Ukraine: The Constitutional Politics of State Formation*, Central European Press, 2002.

Wolchik, S.L. and Zviglyanich, V., (eds.), *Ukraine: The Search for a National Identity*, Lanham, MA: Rowman and Littlefield, 2000.

Wurm, S.A., "Languages in Danger. The Life and Death of the World's Languages", *Multiethnica*, 24-25, 1999: 28-35.

Zhurzhenko, T., "The myth of two Ukraines", can be found at www.eurozine.com, downloaded 25 September 2004.

Zhurzhenko, T., "Part 1: Cross-border Cooperation and Transformation of Regional Identities in the Ukrainian-Russian Borderlands: Towards a Euroregion 'Slobozhanshchina'", *Nationalities Papers*, 32, 1, March 2004: 207-231.

Russian and Ukrainian Language Sources

Chizhikova, L., "Russko-ukrainskoe pogranich'e: istoriia i sud'by traditsionno-bytovoi kul'tury (XIX-XX vv.)", Moscow: *Nauka*, 1988: 14-69.

Danilenko, V, M., Husenkov, S, H., Kolodyazhnyi, N, N., *Istoriia Ukrayiny: 10 klas*, Zaporozh'ye: Prem'er, 2002.

Dontsov, D., *Rosiis'ki vplyvy na ukrayins'ki psykhiku*, Lviv: *Russica*, 1913.

Gordienko, V., *Rabochaya Gazeta*, Kiev, 13 January 1993.

Holovaha, Y. and Panina, N., "Tendentsii Rozvytku Ukrayinsko-Rosiyskykh Vidnosyn u Hromadskyi Dumtsi Rosii ta Ukrayiny", 1998, http://niurr.gov.ua/ukr/zbirka/golovpan.html, quoted in Wolczuk, K., "History, Europe and the 'National Idea'", 671-694.

Horelik, A.F., Virova, T.V., Krasil'nikiv, K.R., *Istoriya ridnoho krayu (Luhans'ka Oblast', Ch 1*, Luhans'k: Luhan', 1995, (History of the native region: Luhans'k region, part 1).

Horelik, A.F., Namdarov, H.M., Bashkina, V.Ya., *Istoriya ridnoho krayu (Luhans'ka Oblast'), Ch.2*, Luhans'k: Luhan', 1997, (History of the native region: Luhans'k region, part 2).

Hryn'ov, V., *Nova Ukrayina: yakoiu ya ii bachu*, Kiev: *Abrys*, 1995.

Hrytsak, Y., "Ukrayina, 1991-1995 rr.: nova politychna natsiia", *Skhid*, 4, 1996.

Hrytsak, Y., "Yak vikladati istoriyu Ukrayini pislya 1991 roky?", *Ukrayins'ka Istorychna Dydaktyka: Mizhnarodni Dialog*, Kiev: Geneza, 2000: 63-75.

Kalendarno-tematichnye planuvannya z Istoriyi Ukrayini, Vsesvitnyoi Istoriyi, Pravozhavstva, za novimi (2001 roku) navchal'nimi prohrami, Zaporizhzhya: Premer', 2001.

Kas'yanov, H., in *Vitchizhyana Istoriya v shkolax i vusax Ukrayini: Octannye desyatyrychchya*, Kiev: Kennan Institute, 2002.

Kononenko, O.E., Shul'zhenko, L.S., *Kharkivshchynoznavstvo*, Kharkiv: Gymnaziya, 2002, (Knowledge about the Kharkiv region).

Kornilov, D.V., "Dukh pereiaslavskoi rady i obshchestvenno-politicheskaia mysl' Ukrayiny kontsa 19-20 veka", *340 rokiv Pereiaslavkoi rady: Mizhnarodna naukova konferentsiia. Tezy dopovidei. Vypusk I*, Donets'k, 1994.

Kul'chyts'kyi, S., Comments in the seminar, "*Vitchiznyana Istoriya v shkolax i vuzax Ukrayiny: Ostannye Desyatyrychchya*", Kiev: Kennan Institute, 2002.

Ladichenko,T.V., Sviderskaya,V.V., Sviderskiy,Y.Y., *Istoriia Ukrayiny; 7 klas*, Zaporozh'ye: Prem'er, 2002.

Leont'eva, H.H., Tuleneva, V.O., Yatsenko, D.I., Cherepanova, E.O., *Heohrafiya ridnoho krayu: 5 klas*, Sumy: Nota bene, 2002: 1-74. (The geography of the native region: 5th Grade).

Malaniuk, I., "Malorosiistvo", NY: *Visnyk*, ODFFU, 1959: 10-13.

Matzing, H. C., "Sotsialystychnye minulye v nimets'kix pidruchnikax- do pytannya pro vivchennya neprostoi temi", in *Ukrayins'ka Istorychna Dydaktyka*, 291-307.

"Navishcho potribna derusifikatsiia Ukrayiny", *Za Vilnu Ukrayinu*, 65, 1993.

"Natsional'nyi sostav naseleniya SSSR po rezultatam vsesouznoj perepisi naselenia 1989", Moscow: *Finansy i Statistika*, 1991.(Ministry of Statistics of the USSR).

Pankrat'ev, O.A., *Heohrafiya ridnoho krayu: Luhans'ka oblast, 5 klas*, Luhans'k: Yantar, 2001. (Geography of the native region: Luhans'k region).

Pas'ko, I., "Natsional'na ideia: varianty na tli ievropeis'koi kul'tury", *Skhid*, 4, 5-6, 1996.

Pogrebinskii, M., (ed.), *Politicheskie nastroeniia nakanune vyborov*, Ukraina, 1997, Kiev: Centre for Political Research and Conflictology, 1997.

"Politichni obrii Luhanshchyni," *Ukrayins'kii rehional'nii visnik*, 38, 1 November 2001, Institut Skhid-Zakhid.

Popov, V., "Prishla pora ob'ediniat'sia", *Brat'ia slaviane*, 9, 1996.

"Pro Natsional'ny doktrinu rozvitku osviti", 347, 17 April, 2002, which can be found at, www.kuchma.gov.ua/main/?whatto-557, accessed 1 March 2005.

Prohrama spetskursi z istorii ta kul'turi ridnoho krayu Luhans'koi oblasti (z naidavnishix chasiv do poch. XXst) dlya uchniv 8-9 klasiv, Luhans'k, 2002.

Ryabchuk, M., *"Vid Malorosii do Ukrayiny. Paradoksy zapizniloho natsiietvorennia"*, Kiev: *Krytyka*, 2000.

Ryabchuk, M., "Dve Ukrayini", Kiev: *Krytyka*, 10, 2001.

Sadkina, V.I., *Geografiya rodnogo kraya, 5 klas*, Khar'kov: Skorpion, 2001. (The geography of the native region: 5th Grade).

Shapoval, Y., in *Vitchizhyana Istoriya v shkolax i vusax Ukrayini: Octannye desyatyrychchya*, Kiev: Kennan Institute, 2002.

Shevchuk, V.P., Taranenko, N.G., Levitas, F.L., Gisem, A,V., *Istoriia Ukrayiny: 11 klas,* Zaporozh'ye: Prem'er, 2001.

Shyl'zhenko, L.S, *Geografiya rodnogo kraya: Slobozhanshchyna, 5 klas,* Khar'kov: Ranok, 2001. (The geography of the native region: Slobozhanshchyna, 5th Grade).

"Sistema osviti v Ukrayini: stan ta perspectivi rosvitku", in *National'na bespeka i oborona,* 4, 28, 2002: 8., Ukrayins'kyi tsentr ekonomichnix i politichnix doslidzhen' imeni Oleksandra Razumkova.

"'Skhidni vorota Ukrayini': kudi voni vedut?", *Ukrayinskii rehional'nii visnik,* 38, 1 November 2001, *Institut Skhid-Zakhid.*

Snezhkova, I.A., "K probleme izuchenia etnicheskogo samosoznani u detei i iunoshestva", *Sovetskaya etnografia,* 1982: 1.

Soldatenko, et al., (eds.), *Ukrayins'ka ideia: pershi rechnyky,* Kiev: Znannia, 1994.

Turchenko, F.H., Moroko, V.N., *Istoriia Ukrayiny: konets XVIII-nachalo XX veka,* Kiev: Geneza, 2001.

Ukrayins'ka Istorychna Dydaktyka: Mizhnarodni Dialog, Kiev:Geneza, 2000.

Vilens'ka, E., Poklad, V., "Natsional'no-kul'turni oriientatsii meshkantsiv Luhans'koi oblasti", *Filosofs'ka i sotsiolohichna dumka,* 4, 1993.

Vlasov, V.S., *Istoriia Ukrayiny: 8 klas,* Kiev: *A.S.K,* 2002.

Zastavnyi, F.D., *"Naselennya Ukrayiny",* Lviv: *Prosvita,* 1993.

Zheleznyi, A., "Ukrayina: kak vozniklo dvuiazychnie", Donetskii kriazh, 18-24 June 1993.

Appendices

This section is divided into two parts. The first part lists the qualitative interviews with education officials, school directors, history teachers and schoolchildren across the three study areas of Luhans'k, Kharkiv and Sumy, from which the vast bulk of empirical data used in this study was generated.

In the group interviews with schoolchildren, in each school, groups numbered between ten and twenty individuals.These interviews took place between January and April 2003. For reasons of anonymity, the full names of interviewees throughout the book have been omitted. Also, for the same reason, the real identities of the schools have been omitted. In each of the study areas, in order to maintain representativeness, the author made sure that the choice of schools was a mix of state and private, Ukrainian and Russian language instruction and located in both central and poorer neighbourhoods of each of the cities. Also are listed interviews which took place with academics in Kiev.

The second part is an example of the set of thematic questions which were asked by the author during the interviews.

APPENDIX I: QUALITATIVE INTERVIEWS

Luhans'k

School 1
- Schoolchildren, Grades 10 and 11, 14 February 2003.
- Ludmilla, School history teacher, 14 February 2003.
- Anatoliy, School director, 19 February 2003
- Anastasiya, School history teacher, 14 February 2003.

School 2
- Schoolchildren, Grades 10 and 11, 24 February 2003.
- Anna, School history teacher, 24 February 2003.
- Elena, School history teacher, 24 February 2003.

School 3
- Schoolchildren, Grades 10 and 11, 5 March 2003
- Grigoriy, School history teacher, 5 March 2003.
- Natal'ya, School history teacher, 5 March 2003.

School No. 4
- Galina, School history teacher, 6 March 2003.
- Olga, former teacher trainer in history at Luhans'k oblast's Institute for Uninterrupted Education, 12th March 2003.

School No.5
- Schoolchildren, Grades 10 and 11, 18 March 2003
- Larisa, School director and history teacher, 18 March 2003.
- Nikolaiy, School history teacher, 18 March 2003.

School No. 6
- Schoolchildren, Grades 10 and 11, 18 March 2003.
- Tatyana, School history teacher, 25 April 2003.
- Irina, School history teacher, 25 April 2003.

Kharkiv

School No. 1
- Schoolchildren, Grades 10 and 11, 3 April 2003.
- School history teacher, 3 April 2003.

School No. 2
- Schoolchildren, Grades 10 and 11, 4 April 2003.
- Taisiya, School history teacher, 4 April 2003.
- Svetlana, School history teacher, 4 April 2003.

School No. 3
- Schoolchildren, Grades 10 and 11, 4 April 2003.
- Lubov', School history teacher, 4 April 2003.
- Elena, School history teacher, 4 April 2003.

School No. 4
- Schoolchildren, Grades 10 and 11, 4 April 2003.
- Grigoriy, School history teacher, 4 April 2003.

School No.5
- Schoolchildren, Grades 10 and 11, March 29 2003.
- Tatyana, School history teacher, 23 March 2003.
- Anatoliy, Reader in pedagogy, 22 March 2003.
- Gennadiy, Assistant director of the faculty of history and political science, 23 March 2003.
- Ekaterina, School history teacher, 22 March 2003.

Kharkiv State University
- Chorniy, Dmitri Nikolaiyevich, Senior lecturer of 'Ukrainian studies' faculty, 20 March 2003.

Kharkiv City Council
- Lytsenko, Aleksandr Sergeevich, Vice-director of Education Department, 7 April 2003.

Kharkiv Oblast's Centre for Uninterrupted Education
- Oksana, Methodologist at Kharkiv Oblast's Centre for Uninterrupted Education, 7 April 2003.

Sumy

School No. 1
- Schoolchildren, Grades 10 and 11, 18 April 2003.
- Valentina, School history teacher, 18 April 2003.

School No. 2
- Schoolchildren, Grades 10 and 11, 18 April 2003.
- Oksana, School history teacher, 18 April 2003.
- Tamara, School history teacher, 18 April 2003.
- Irina, School history teacher, 18 April 2003.

School No.3
- Schoolchildren, Grades 10 and 11, 18 April 2003.
- School history teacher, 18 April 2003.

School No. 4
- Schoolchildren, Grades 10 and 11, 19 April 2003.
- School history teacher, 19 April 2003.

School No.5
- Schoolchildren, Grades 10 and 11, 19 April 2003.
- School history teacher, 19 April 2003.

Kiev

- Hryhoriy Nemyria, Director of the Centre for European and International Studies, 28 January 2003.
- Georgij Kasianov, Education Programs Director, International Renaissance Foundation, 28 January 2003.

APPENDIX II: INTERVIEW QUESTIONS

- What changes have taken place in the 'History of Ukraine' course since 1991?

- What do you think about these changes?

- How does today's History of Ukraine course compare with the history course, taught inthe Soviet period?

- What specific parts of today's 'History of Ukraine' course do you like? Why?

- What specific parts of today's 'History of Ukraine' course do you not like? Why?

- What do you feel about the depiction of the period of Kiev Rus' in the new Ukrainian textbooks?

- What do you feel about the depiction of the role of the Hetmans Khmelnyt-sk'yi and Mazepa in the new Ukrainian textbooks?

- How do you think the Soviet years are represented in the new Ukrainian textbooks?

- What do you feel about the depiction of the 'Great Famine' in the new Ukrainian textbooks?

- What do you feel about the depiction of the war years between 1941-1945 in the new Ukrainian textbooks?

- How do you think that Russia and Russians are represented in the 'History of Ukraine' course?

It needs to be reiterated, as previously outlined in the methodological Chapter, these questions were not all used and in this order, in a 'list format' during each interview. Rather they acted as a 'guide' for the author. Thus, in different interviews, depending on the interaction between the interviewer and interviewee(s), various topics were given greater or less attention. At all times, the author tried to allow the interviewees to have 'their voice' heard, dictating the pace and content of each interview themselves, to a certain degree.

SOVIET AND POST-SOVIET POLITICS AND SOCIETY

Edited by Dr. Andreas Umland

ISSN 1614-3515

75 Heiko Pleines (Hrsg.)
Corporate Governance in post-
sozialistischen Volkswirtschaften
ISBN 978-3-89821-766-8

76 Stefan Ihrig
Wer sind die Moldawier?
Rumänismus versus Moldowanismus in
Historiographie und Schulbüchern der
Republik Moldova, 1991-2006
Mit einem Vorwort von Holm Sundhaussen
ISBN 978-3-89821-466-7

77 Galina Kozhevnikova in collaboration
with Alexander Verkhovsky and
Eugene Veklerov
Ultra-Nationalism and Hate Crimes in
Contemporary Russia
The 2004-2006 Annual Reports of Moscow's
SOVA Center
With a foreword by Stephen D. Shenfield
ISBN 978-3-89821-868-9

78 Florian Küchler
The Role of the European Union in
Moldova's Transnistria Conflict
With a foreword by Christopher Hill
ISBN 978-3-89821-850-4

79 Bernd Rechel
The Long Way Back to Europe
Minority Protection in Bulgaria
With a foreword by Richard Crampton
ISBN 978-3-89821-863-4

80 Peter W. Rodgers
Nation, Region and History in Post-
Communist Transitions
Identity Politics in Ukraine, 1991-2006
With a foreword by Vera Tolz
ISBN 978-3-89821-903-7

FORTHCOMING (MANUSCRIPT
WORKING TITLES)

Stephanie Solowyda
Biography of Semen Frank
ISBN 3-89821-457-5

Margaret Dikovitskaya
Arguing with the Photographs
Russian Imperial Colonial Attitudes in Visual Culture
ISBN 3-89821-462-1

Sergei M. Plekhanov
Russian Nationalism in the Age of
Globalization
ISBN 3-89821-484-2

Robert Pyrah
Cultural Memory and Identity
Literature, Criticism and the Theatre in Lviv - Lwow -
Lemberg, 1918-1939 and in post-Soviet Ukraine
ISBN 3-89821-505-9

Andrei Rogatchevski
The National-Bolshevik Party
ISBN 3-89821-532-6

Zenon Victor Wasyliw
Soviet Culture in the Ukrainian Village
The Transformation of Everyday Life and Values,
1921-1928
ISBN 3-89821-536-9

Nele Sass
Das gegenkulturelle Milieu im
postsowjetischen Russland
ISBN 3-89821-543-1

Julie Elkner
Maternalism versus Militarism
The Russian Soldiers' Mothers Committee
ISBN 3-89821-575-X

Alexandra Kamarowsky
Russia's Post-crisis Growth
ISBN 3-89821-580-6

Martin Friessnegg
Das Problem der Medienfreiheit in Russland
seit dem Ende der Sowjetunion
ISBN 3-89821-588-1

Nikolaj Nikiforowitsch Borobow
Führende Persönlichkeiten in Russland vom
12. bis 20 Jhd.: Ein Lexikon
Aus dem Russischen übersetzt und herausgegeben von
Eberhard Schneider
ISBN 3-89821-638-1

Martin Malek, Anna Schor-Tschudnowskaja
Tschetschenien und die Gleichgültigkeit
Europas
Russlands Kriege und die Agonie der Idee der
Menschenrechte
ISBN 3-89821-676-4

Andreas Langenohl
Political Culture and Criticism of Society
Intellectual Articulations in Post-Soviet Russia
ISBN 3-89821-709-4

Thomas Borén
Meeting Places in Transformation
ISBN 3-89821-739-6

Lars Löckner
Sowjetrussland in der Beurteilung der
Emigrantenzeitung 'Rul', 1920-1924
ISBN 3-89821-741-8

Ekaterina Taratuta
The Red Line of Construction
Semantics and Mythology of a Siberian Heliopolis
ISBN 3-89821-742-6

Bernd Kappenberg
Zeichen setzen für Europa
Der Gebrauch europäischer lateinischer Sonderzeichen
in der deutschen Öffentlichkeit
ISBN 3-89821-749-3

*Siegbert Klee, Martin Sandhop, Oxana
Schwajka, Andreas Umland*
Elitenbildung in der Postsowjetischen
Ukraine
ISBN 978-389821-829-0

Natalya Ketenci
The effect of location on the performance of
Kazakhstani industrial enterprises in the
transition period
ISBN 978-389821-831-3

Quotes from reviews of SPPS volumes:

On vol. 1 – *The Implementation of the ECHR in Russia*: "Full of examples, experiences and valuable observations which could provide the basis for new strategies."
Diana Schmidt, *Неприкосновенный запас*, 2005

On vol. 2 – *Putins Russland*: "Wipperfürth draws attention to little known facts. For instance, the Russians have still more positive feelings towards Germany than to any other non-Slavic country."
Oldag Kaspar, *Süddeutsche Zeitung, 2005*

On vol. 3 – *Die Übernahme internationalen Rechts in die russische Rechtsordnung*: "Hussner's is an interesting, detailed and, at the same time, focused study which deals with all relevant aspects and contains insights into contemporary Russian legal thought."
Herbert Küpper, *Jahrbuch für Ostrecht, 2005*

On vol. 5 – *Квадратные метры, определяющие сознание*: „Meerovich provides a study that will be of considerable value to housing specialists and policy analysts."
Christina Varga-Harris, *Slavic Review, 2006*

On vol. 6 – *New Directions in Russian International Studies*: "A helpful step in the direction of an overdue dialogue between Western and Russian IR scholarly communities."
Diana Schmidt, *Europe-Asia Studies, 2006*

On vol. 8 – *Nation-Building and Minority Politics in Post-Socialist States:* "Galbreath's book is an admirable and craftsmanlike piece of work, and should be read by all specialists interested in the Baltic area."
Andrejs Plakans, *Slavic Review, 2007*

On vol. 9 – *Народы Кавказа в Вооружённых силах СССР:* "In this superb new book, Bezugolnyi skillfully fashions an accurate and candid record of how and why the Soviet Union mobilized and employed the various ethnic groups in the Caucasus region in the Red Army's World War II effort."
David J. Glantz, *Journal of Slavic Military Studies, 2006*

On vol. 10 – *Русское Национальное Единство*: "Pribylovskii's and Likhachev's work is likely to remain the definitive study of the Russian National Unity for a very long time."
Mischa Gabowitsch, *e-Extreme, 2006*

On vol. 13 – *The Politicization of Russian Orthodoxy*: "Mitrofanova's book is a fascinating study which raises important questions about the type of national ideology that will come to predominate in the new Russia."
Zoe Knox, *Europe-Asia Studies, 2006*

On vol. 14 – *Aleksandr Solzhenitsyn and the Modern Russo-Jewish Question*: "Larson has written a well-balanced survey of Solzhenitsyn's writings on Russian-Jewish relations."
Nikolai Butkevich, *e-Extreme, 2006*

On vol. 16 – *Der russische Sonderweg?:* "Luks's remarkable knowledge of the history of this wide territory from the Elbe to the Pacific Ocean and his life experience give his observations a particular sharpness and his judgements an exceptional weight."

Peter Krupnikow, *Mitteilungen aus dem baltischen Leben*, 2006

On vol. 17 – *История «Мёртвой воды»:* "Moroz provides one of the best available surveys of Russian neo-paganism."

Mischa Gabowitsch, *e-Extreme*, 2006

On vol. 18 – *Этническая и религиозная интолерантность в российских СМИ:* "A constructive contribution to a crucial debate about media-endorsed intolerance which has once again flared up in Russia."

Mischa Gabowitsch, *e-Extreme*, 2006

On vol. 25 – *The Ghosts in Our Classroom:* "Freyberg-Inan's well-researched and incisive monograph, balanced and informed about Romanian education in general, should be required reading for those Eurocrats who have shaped Romanian spending priorities since 2000."

Tom Gallagher, *Slavic Review*, 2006

On vol. 26 – *The 2002 Dubrovka and 2004 Beslan Hostage Crises:* "Dunlop's analysis will help to draw Western attention to the plight of those who have suffered by these terrorist acts, and the importance, for all Russians, of uncovering the truth of about what happened."

Amy Knight, *Times Literary Supplement*, 2006

On vol. 29 – *Zivilgesellschaftliche Einflüsse auf die Orange Revolution:* „Strasser's study constitutes an outstanding empirical analysis and well-grounded location of the subject within theory."

Heiko Pleines, *Osteuropa*, 2006

On vol. 34 – *Postsowjetische Feiern:* "Mühlfried's book contains not only a solid ethnographic study, but also points at some problems emerging from Georgia's prevalent understanding of culture."

Godula Kosack, *Anthropos*, 2007

On vol. 35 – *Fascism Past and Present, West and East:* "Committed students will find much of interest in these sometimes barbed exchanges."

Robert Paxton, *Journal of Global History*, 2007

On vol. 37 – *Political Anti-Semitism in Post-Soviet Russia:* "Likhachev's book serves as a reliable compendium and a good starting point for future research on post-Soviet xenophobia and ultra-nationalist politics, with their accompanying anti-Semitism."

Kathleen Mikkelson, *Demokratizatsiya*, 2007

Series Subscription

Please enter my subscription to the series *Soviet and Post-Soviet Politics and Society*, ISSN 1614-3515, as follows:

❏ complete series   OR   ❏ English-language titles
                                                      ❏ German-language titles
                                                      ❏ Russian-language titles

starting with
❏ volume # 1
❏ volume # ___
     ❏ please also include the following volumes: #___, ___, ___, ___, ___, ___, ___
❏ the next volume being published
     ❏ please also include the following volumes: #___, ___, ___, ___, ___, ___, ___

❏ 1 copy per volume   OR   ❏ ___ copies per volume

Subscription within Germany:
You will receive every volume at 1st publication at the regular bookseller's price – incl. s & h and VAT.
Payment:
❏ Please bill me for every volume.
❏ Lastschriftverfahren: Ich/wir ermächtige(n) Sie hiermit widerruflich, den Rechnungsbetrag je Band von meinem/unserem folgendem Konto einzuziehen.

Kontoinhaber: _____Kreditinstitut: _____
Kontonummer: _____Bankleitzahl:_____

International Subscription:
Payment (incl. s & h and VAT) in advance for
❏ 10 volumes/copies (€ 319.80)   ❏ 20 volumes/copies (€ 599.80)
❏ 40 volumes/copies (€ 1,099.80)
Please send my books to:

NAME_____DEPARTMENT_____
ADDRESS _____
POST/ZIP CODE_____COUNTRY _____
TELEPHONE _____EMAIL_____

date/signature_____

A hint for librarians in the former Soviet Union: Your academic library might be eligible to receive free-of-cost scholarly literature from Germany via the German Research Foundation. For Russian-language information on this program, see
http://www.dfg.de/forschungsfoerderung/formulare/download/12_54.pdf.

Please fax to: **0511 / 262 2201 (+49 511 262 2201)**
or mail to: *ibidem*-Verlag, Julius-Leber-Weg 11, D-30457 Hannover,Germany
or send an e-mail: ibidem@ibidem-verlag.de

ibidem-Verlag

Melchiorstr. 15

D-70439 Stuttgart

info@ibidem-verlag.de

www.ibidem-verlag.de
www.edition-noema.de
www.autorenbetreuung.de

www.ingramcontent.com/pod-product-compliance
Lightning Source LLC
Chambersburg PA
CBHW050708280326
41926CB00088B/2878